Frank D. Carpenter

The Wonders of Geyser Land

A Trip to the Yellowstone National Park of Wyoming

Frank D. Carpenter

The Wonders of Geyser Land
A Trip to the Yellowstone National Park of Wyoming

ISBN/EAN: 9783337145385

Printed in Europe, USA, Canada, Australia, Japan

Cover: Foto ©Andreas Hilbeck / pixelio.de

More available books at **www.hansebooks.com**

THE WONDERS

—OF—

GEYSER LAND.

A TRIP TO THE

YELLOWSTONE NATIONAL PARK,

OF WYOMING.

Together with a thrilling account of the

Capture By The Nez Perces Indians,

AND SUBSEQUENT ESCAPE OF THE

NATIONAL PARK TOURISTS,

Of Radersburg and Helena, Montana, in August, 1877.

ILLUSTRATED.

By F. D. CARPENTER,

SON OF D. D. CARPENTER, FORMERLY OF WISCONSIN.

BLACK EARTH, WIS.:
BURNETT & SON, PRINTERS AND PUBLISHERS.
1878.

WONDERS OF GEYSER LAND.

Having heard of the curiosities of Wonderland, and being impelled with a desire to view them for myself, I resolved, in July of 1877, that I would visit them. I consulted with a friend, Mr. A. Oldham, who, also was anxious to behold the beauties of this wonderful region, and we concluded to make immediate preparations for our departure. We accordingly each procured a saddle horse and a pack animal and expected to complete our preparations and be upon the road by the 1st of August.

A few days previous to the time of our contemplated departure, however, I met Mr. A. J. Arnold, of Blackfoot, who, upon being informed that Mr. Oldham and myself were about ready to start for the Geysers or National Park, said that if we would wait until he could complete his preparations he would accompany us. Being glad of his company we consented to do so, and then, since there were three of us, we altered our plans as to the manner of our going and procured a buggy.

Having completed our arrangements and purchased provisions for a six weeks camp, we left Helena on the 29th of July for my father's who resided about forty-five miles from Helena, on a small stream call Deep Creek, that empties into the Missouri River, where we proposed procuring other necessaries for the trip. Here I saw my brother-in-law, George F. Cowan, who said he would go with us, as also did Charles Mann, of Radeisburg. William Dingee, of Helena, having expressed a desire to be one of the party we concluded that we would organize a larger party than we at first proposed doing and made preparations accordingly. Mrs. Cowan, my sister, and a younger sister, Ida, aged thirteen years, concluded that they would like to join the party, and a great many others said they would go with us if we would wait ten or fifteen days, but as business required that most of us be back by the first of September, we could wait no longer, and on the third day of August, having borrowed a team from my father and secured the services of a young man, named Henry Myers to take charge of it, we drove down to the river and crossed at Indian Creek Ferry.

Having crossed the river we went to Radersburg, a distance of eighteen miles from my father's where we arrived at two o'clock in the afternoon. Here Mr. Cowan, Mrs. Cowan and Mr. Mann were to join us, but being informed by them that they would not be ready for two or three days, we, with the characteristic *sang froid* of the western people, though anxious to be off, made ourselves at home.

On the 5th we bade farewell to our friends and were soon on our journey southward. I will now quote from my journal which was kept from the time of our departure until our capture by the Indians. The journal was left in the buggy at the time of our capture, and was picked up by Mr. Cowan as he was returning towards the Geyser Basin after being wounded by the Indians.

SUNDAY, AUGUST 5th.—Left Radersburg in the morning and proceeded two miles to Crow Creek, where we halted to make some preparations that we had forgotten. At 10 30 we left Crow Creek and a drive of nine miles brought us to the place of Mr. Naves. Here we halted to await the return of Cowan who had gone to the residence of a man, named Wilson, to borrow a needle gun. Upon his return we proceeded along the "divide" that separates the valley of Crow Creek from that of Jefferson River, a distance of twenty-two miles from Radersburg. As we were leisurely wending our way up the divide at a distance of four or five miles from Naves', and when near the summit of a rise, we suddenly espied three antelope lying in the road about three hundred yards ahead of us. As we approached they jumped to their feet and stood gazing at us as if not at all frightened. Here was meat for the larder, and we halted to give our marksmen an opportunity to secure it. With the confidence of old hunters they dismounted and after a brief parley as to whom should the honor of "first game" be given, one of our nimrods took deliberate aim, fired—and the antelope looked somewhat surprised at the noise. Another marksman stepped to the front with the utmost assurance, took a long and deadly aim, fired—and the antelope began to move off. A half dozen shots were fired in quick succession, and the antelope, in honor to the salute, paused for an instant in graceful recognition and bounded away. As a matter of course, the guns were to blame.

Arriving at the top of the divide we struck a livelier gait and proceeded down the other side at about eight miles an hour. When near the foot of the hill, I found I had lost my hat and the prospects for a bare headed campaign were imminent. Fortunately Mr. Mann had an extra one that he gave me. We arrived at the Jefferson River at about 7 P. M. and went into camp about two miles from its confluence with the Missouri.

We had encamped near a ranche, and during the interval of supper getting, which the male portion of the party had gallantly taken upon themselves, Emma and Ida went over to it for the purpose of making the acquaintance of the inmates. They were agreeably surprised to find that persons occupying it were old acquaintances of the Cowans, by the name of Crab, who had but recently married and moved here from Radersburg. They accepted an invitation to remain for supper, and afterwards returned to camp with an invitation for the whole company to spend the evening with their new found friends.

During the absence of the ladies we were busily engaged in preparing our first meal in camp, and at the usual mountain signal for refreshments, "grub pile," we proceeded to lighten the stock of provisions by a hundred pounds or less. As the meal progressed, Dingee, who was as yet fastidious, remarked that he would "fall off twenty pounds in weight before his return," and subsequent events prove the truthfulness of the prediction, but in a way not anticipated by him. Having finished the frugal repast Dingee said he "did not feel well," and in view of the quantity of provisions consumed by him it created no astonishment in the minds of the party.

Supper over, we took a guitar and violin and with the exception of Dingee, who volunteered to act as dishwasher for the occasion, repaired to the hospitable roof of the Crabs, where we passed a pleasant evening in music and song. The hour of eleven came speedily, and leaving Emma and Ida to remain over night we returned to camp. As we approached we were astonished at the appearance of Dingee, who apparently was endeavoring (as the boys put it) "to skin a cat through his mouth." He didn't look well, and an expression of ineffable disgust swept over his features when interrogated as to his "feelings." We spread our blankets on the green sward, and in a few minutes were dreaming of the geysers, the idea of which was suggested, I presume, by the recent spoutings of Dingee and the gentle rumblings of his snores.

August 6th.—At day break Dingee, having fully recovered, was up calling all hands to "grub," and it may be presumed that we did ample justice to his bill of fare. After breakfast Cowan started down the river to get a tent at a place where Crab told us one could be obtained, and the ballance of the party struck out on the road.

We crossed the river by a bridge, and beyond a slough close to the river, we came to Shed's toll bridge, about a mile and a half from camp. We turned southward, and as we were driving close to the river I had the good fortune to get three large mallard ducks that furnished an ample supply of the choicest meat for dinner. About eight miles up the valley we saw antelope in the distance, and although Mr. Oldham and myself tried for a shot we were unsuccessful. We turned up Willow Creek, where we were to wait for Cowan and the buggy. Here the residents kindly informed us that the Indians would capture us, but thinking there was no immediate danger at least, we pushed onward leaving the Jefferson to the right. At Fredrick's mill, sixteen miles from our camp of the night previous, we stopped for dinner. Mrs. F. wished to join our party, but as she could not get ready inside of two days we decided to go ahead, and increasing our larder by the addition of two sacks of flour which we purchased from Mr. Fredricks we resumed our journey.

At Sterling, a mining town in the mountains, situated on Meadow Creek, twenty-six miles from Fredrick's, night overtook us and we stopped and went into camp. The "grub wagon," which we were momentarily expecting did not come and most of the party retired supperless. Cowan said that he would not go without supper if he had to wait till breakfast time, so we waited hungrily until midnight, when the rattle of wheels told of their arrival and shortly after we were busily engaged in appeasing our inordinate appetites.

AUGUST 7th,—Broke camp at eight o'clock and bade farewell to the desolated city of Sterling, which like many other mining cities, is one of the things that were. From Sterling we crossed Madison "divide" at a point where it is twelve miles from water to water. Near the summit Mr. Oldham and myself, being in advance, descried more antelope about a half mile below the road, and we determined to try our luck with the guns that had so cruelly deceived the others. I returned to the wagon for my gun, but Mr. Cowan expressing a desire to try a shot, I gave him my horse and gun, and he and Mr. Oldham started in quest of the game.

We drove down the divide, and coming to a pretty little brook that was alive with trout, we stopped for dinner. We turned up the stream to a point about a mile above the road, and halted for the "grub wagon, which, as before, we had left in charge of Myers and Mann. It came in sight, and passed us despite the yelling of the whole party. They did not hear us, and I started after them on foot. After a vigorous walk of two miles, I overtook them and turned them back into camp.

Cowan and Oldham came in sight, and we succeeded in making

them hear us and shortly afterwards they rode into camp, bringing with them the hind quarters of an antelope. (It may be noted their good luck was not accredited to the guns.) At three P. M. we were on the road again, and after a pleasant drive of fifteen miles across the bench, we halted for night. As usual, our provisions were behind, and as we were out fishing when it passed, the prospect for supper was poor indeed. On mounting a bridge which spans the Madison near where we camped, I could see the wagon fading in the dim distance. Hastily dispatching one of the party in pursuit on a horse, we, in the course of an hour or so were enjoying an excellent supper, to which a fine lot of brook trout added not a little. Here, again, Dingee expressed fears relative to his anticipated "falling off" in flesh, but the party could not agree with him, inasmuch as his horse had to carry the amount that he ate. Supper over, we passed the evening in music and song, and at eleven, "turned in" for the night.

August 8th.—The sun rose bright and clear, and this promises to be a beautiful day. We were on the move at eight o'clock. We cross the bridge and the river bottom beyond, and about a mile from camp, strike the bench land again. We now have a beautiful drive up the Madison: the roads are good, and the party in excellent spirits, (or the spirits in them 95 per cent. proof.) We drove twenty miles, and camped for noon, on Bear Creek. Here we met a herder hunting horses, of whom we asked how far we had come since morning. We had been traveling at a lively gate all the forenoon, and one may rest assured that thanks were not pleasantly returned, when he informed us we had come but eight miles. Oldham observed that "he looked like a man of truth, but that he'd bet he had lied by about twelve miles by the watch," and a reference to our guide book, showed that we had driven eighteen miles. We also found that by driving eight miles farther, we would strike a small stream, called Indian Creek, so we concluded that we would not camp for noon, but drive on to the creek and camp for the night.

After leaving Bear Creek, there was no timber, and we were

compelled to follow cow paths for a distance of ten miles, where we left the bench and drove down to a pretty stream that we rightly conjectured, was Indian Creek. We drove down the stream for a mile and selected a beautiful camping place. We had here, fine sport fishing, and Cowan shot some nice sage hens, and a couple of large bald headed eagles.

From our position, looking down towards the mountains, we saw, about ten miles away, what we supposed were a number of Indian ponies. Thinking to be on our guard, Dingee and myself started out to scout. We passed down the creek three or four miles, struck off to the right, and came out about two miles below the objects that had excited such a warm interest. We cautiously approached, and on gaining an eminence, where we had an unobstructed view, found the objects of suspicion were an herd of cattle. We silently looked at each other, shook hands, called it "draw game," and returned to camp to relate the result, and allay the fears of the party. As usual, the evening was passed in song, and after Mr. Mann had sketched the party and camp, we retired for the night.

AUGUST 9.—Again the weather is beautiful. Breakfast over, we "hitch up," and start up the creek, which we follow a mile and a half, when we strike a trail leading up the Madison, which we take. We follow this for twelve miles, then turn abruptly towards the river, and proceed about two miles, when we strike a little stream, where we camped for dinner. Arnold, Myers, and myself, went to the river, where we caught some fine trout, while the others were getting dinner and picking berries.

At 3 P. M. we are again on the road, and follow the trail as before. The path becomes more distinct as we proceed, and finally emerges into a good road. The road follows close by the river, and we follow it for a distance of ten miles, or to a point where a large stream, from the south-west, empties into it. This stream, just above its junction with the river, flows between two large mountains of rock, and through a dark, deep canyon, that is extremely picturesque. We crossed the Madison, picketed our horses, and after a time spent in fishing, with excellent results, as each took a large string of trout, we partook of a hearty supper and "turned in."

AUGUST 10.—We "rout out," as usual, to the melodious cry of "all hands on deck and "grub pile." An examination of the buggy reveals the fact that we must set the tire ere we go farther. We collect wood, and carry water for the purpose, and soon finish the job, in true western style of "good, if not so nice," and again set out. We follow the south bank of the river, which here flows from the south-east. The scenery is wild and beautiful, the river falls about four feet to the mile, with little ripples running clear across it, here and there, for a distance of about five miles, and the drive was a delightful one. We follow the river for about twelve miles, to second canyon, where it flows out of the mountains. Here we saw little cascades falling, far up the side of the mountains, for a distance of three to five hundred feet. Sparkling in the sun, they looked like threads of silver, and with their back-ground of dark green verdure, were beautiful indeed. Our road now turns abruptly to the south, and we leave the Madison, and start to cross the divide towards Henry's Lake, a distance of ten miles. To the left, the mountains tower away among the clouds, and on the right lies a rolling mountainous country. Antelope and small game are occasionally seen by the road but we do not try for a shot. A pleasant drive of fifteen miles brings us to the top of the divide, and as we look southward we see below us, glistening in the bright sunlight like a mirror, a beautiful sheet of water, dotted here and there with little islands of green. Pelicans, swans, sea gulls and geese, floated upon its surface. We gaze enraptured on this beautiful scene, then, with a shout, drive pell mell towards it.

We came to the north-east end of the lake and passed on up the west side where we found a good camping ground near the ranch of a Mr. Sawtell, which was then unoccupied. We found boats moored near us, and Arnold, Oldham, Ida and myself, started to visit an island about a mile from shore. As we rowed out we saw some fine trout below us that were distinctly visible through the clear water, and swimming near us, we saw a number of swans with their young. On the island we discovered that we had found a hatching place of wild fowls. We named the island, as does every one that visits it. As we returned, Ida threw a line over the stern of the boat and trolled for trout. She soon hooked a large salmon trout, and removing it from the hook took three more ere we reached the shore. Arriving at camp we find that the provisions are again behind, and at dark, the wagon not yet coming, Mr. Cowan mounts a horse and starts in quest of it. He returns shortly, having found it, and we soon partake of a bounteous supper.

Our camp is delightfully situated about three hundred yards from the lake on the mountain side, and we have a beautiful view of it as it lies calmly sleeping in the moonlight. After supper the guitar and violin are brought out and we passed a jolly evening. Mr. Dingee performing some astonishing feats which he denominated "double shuffle" and "pigeon wing," and Mr. Oldham giving vent to the poetry in his nature through the medium of " Where now is them good old prophets?" At eleven Dingee announced the circus closed until the next evening and we went to sleep with plans fully matured for to-morrow's explorations.

During the night the wild birds on the lake, kept up a continual chorus of discordant sounds, swans, pelicans, cranes, and geese vieing with each other in their efforts to make night hideous.

AUGUST 11th.—Dingee's hungry whoop called us from dreamland to the realization of a beautiful morning and ravenous appetites for the excellent breakfast that he had as usual prepared. During the progress of the meal he again complained of "falling off," and the party imposed such confidence in his predictions as to offer him two hundred dollars to return home and thus keep us from actual starvation. He promptly declined.

In accordance with the arrangements of the night previous, the party separated, each to seek such pleasure as his taste dictated.

Cowan, accompanied by Mrs. Cowan, went in quest of deer or elk on the surrounding mountains, Myers and Mann took the smaller of the boats and rowed out upon the lake, as the latter wished to make some sketches, and the remainder of us concluded to visit the head waters of Snake River, the outlet of the lake. We put aboard our guns, ammunition and fishing tackle, provided an ample dinner for Dingee and the rest of the party, and shoved off for a day's cruise.

Arnold and Dingee laid claim to being "old salts," by the reason of their having been born upon the sea-shore, and proceeded to extemporize a sail from an old straw-tick, which we had with us. Oldham and myself, being nothing but "land lubbers," could not participate in the preparations, but, nevertheless, noted them with interest, as we saw in their completion and application an entire absence of back aches and blisters.

The preparations completed, Skippers Dingee and Arnold, with frequent reference to their "timbers," which they re-iterated should be "shivered," and other harder but equally as choice expletives, gave command: "On deck everybody!" and we "shipped oars." The breeze was not sufficiently strong to move us, and we "out oars" again and paddled. Dingee, after the manner of other sailors, when becalmed, stuck his jack-knife into the mast and swore, yet it brought no wind. We took in sail, and rowed toward the east side of the lake, shooting at swan as we passed, but with no success. When nearly across, a fine breeze struck us, and Skipper Dingee gave orders to hoist sail by the seaman-like command, "Sail histed!" We obeyed instantly, and came near upsetting the boat, but soon succeeded in getting before the wind, and made a delightful run to the south end of the lake. As we neared the end of the lake, we saw two swans with their young, which were about as large as wild geese, swimming near us. We approached nearer, and the old ones flew, but we were satisfied with the young ones, five of which we shot, and one we captured alive.

We made the head of the river and landed. We strolled down the river some two miles searching for a good fishing ground, and occasionally getting a shot at some geese, or an antelope on the opposite side of the river. We succeeded only in enjoying ourselves.

We spent the day in rambling aimlessly around, after the manner of a picnic, and towards evening returned to the boat. The wind being "dead ahead," we manned the oars and pulled for camp, keeping close in shore. As we passed some bushes on the bank, the hungry eyes of Dingee discovered some black currants, and we must, of necessity, stop and pick a few. They grew in profusion and were very large. We picked an immense quantity; at least this is the inference from Dingee's asserting that " he had enough." The wind was now blowing strong, and paddling was no recreation. We soon tired of it, when Dingee asserted that he could sail up. We doubted it; but our doubts were partially removed by his self-confident assertion, " that anybody could do it who only knew how." We stood in awe of his superior knowledge, and gazed in silent admiration upon the man as he set the sail and quietly took the helm. The first "tack" brought us back to the river, and filled the boat one-third full of water. Attributing his ill-success to the *fresh water*, he ordered us to shorten sail by the command, " Take down the ―― thing," which we did. On being asked if " we should paddle now or steam up," he lapsed into silence, and gave command to the "land lubbers."

A two hours' hard pull brought us to our landing, and each taking a swan on his back, proceeded single file to camp, where we found all assembled, busily engaged in getting supper. Supper over, we passed the evening in narrating the day's adventures and music. The time for retiring soon came, when we sang our midnight yell, in which Oldham musically queried as to the whereabouts of the "prophets," and retired.

AUGUST 12.—The usual yell of Dingee, that summons us to " grub pile," but which never grows monotonous, again, salutes us as we turn out at the break of day. We find Dingee " heels over head " in dough; we commiserate his condition, and make haste to assist him. We soon sit down to a breakfast of ducks, fish, ham, potatoes, buscuit and canned fruits, and envy not a king his delicacies.

After breakfast we employ the time in skinning our swans, each taking one and dressing it to suit himself. It being Sunday, we concluded to remain in camp, but Mrs. Cowan, who had not, as yet, been on the lake, expressing a desire to go boating, we again manned the boats for another excursion. Skipper Dingee being satisfied with his nautical experiences of the day before, (and so were we) remained in camp, and we could see him sitting on the bank, peacefully smoking his pipe as we pulled away. Before going, however, we asked his advice relative to handling the craft while on a "tack," and also for an explanation of the expression " luff, luff;" which some of the party had construed into " duff," (a seaman's pudding). He abruptly arose and told us " to take a walk," which we did—towards the boats.

We rowed about, fishing for a time; but, growing tired of this sport, pulled towards some swans that were a short distance from us. Mr. Cowan tried a long shot and hit an old one in the neck. We pulled along side of it, and, with no little trouble, succeeded in getting it into the boat. It was one of the largest birds we had ever seen, measuring eight and a half feet from tip to tip. As there were a number of young ones near, we gave chase to capture one, and, after an hour's paddling, succeeded in tiring it out and taking it captive. As we returned to camp, we secured a number of ducks, with but little effort, as they were easily approached, and rowed ashore about four o'clock. Myers and Mann soon appeared in the small boat, bringing with them sevearl large strings of trout. Some of them weighed eight pounds each.

We turned the captive swan loose in camp, and despite the remonstrances of Cowan's dog, Dido, who wished to show off her good qualities, it waddled around the camp as we ate, the while eyeing us suspiciously. I wished to keep it, but finally agreed to return it to the lake, upon the party's agreeing that they would help me catch another on our return. (It may here be noted that we did not all return this way, and those that did were in a hurry.)

After supper Cowan removed the skin of the dead swan and the balance of the party prepared a quantity of fish to carry with us to the geyser basin, distant thirty-five miles.

As we were about to retire, Arnold and Myers said they had found an inviting hay-loft near the ranch, and proposed that we take up our quarters there. Cowan would not move his tent, as he had it cosily prepared, but the remainder of us took our blankets and accepted the hospitality of the loft. As we entered we found some spears, used in fishing, and Arnold, Myers and myself thought to avail ourselves of the pleasure thus offered us, and we started for a torch-light fish. We had a pleasant time for a half-hour, spearing in that time some thirty-five salmon-trout. The wind arose and we returned to bed. My partner for the night was Mr. Oldham, and as I crept in beside him I thought the bed seemed rather hard and cold. Soon I heard complaints from the others, and after a night's fitful dozing, we arose to find we had taken possession of Sawtell's ice-house, and had made our beds on the ice. We were soon in camp, and were not in anywise provoked to find that Cowan and the ladies had already prepared breakfast for us.

AUGUST 13.—At nine o'clock we are again *en route* for geyser land. The road winds around the mountains that border the north-east shore of the lake, and as we reach an eminence at the north end, the lake lies 500 feet below us. From this point we have a most delightful view, and our artist produces his sketch book and outlines it. We halt for a time, and gaze in silent admiration upon the exquisitely beautiful scene. We are loth to leave, and it is with no little regret that we turn mountainward and resume our journey.

We now pass southeast, leaving the lake to the right and in the rear of us, and soon arrive at the mouth of the Targee Pass, and begin the ascent of the mountain. The pass through this mountain is an easy drive, rising gradually for about ten miles. Here we came to a large spring, and stop for dinner in a grove of cotton-wood trees. We get dinner, leave our marks upon the trees with date, and at 2 P. M. are in the saddle. A ride of two miles brings us to the summit of the pass, and thence we gradually descend to a low marshy prairie. Crossing this, which is about eight miles wide, we come to a large stream flowing from the mountains to the south of us, which we suppose is the right fork of the Madison, the water of which we find is quite warm. It is too early to camp, so we push onward. As we jog slowly along, a large herd of antelope cross the road directly in front of us, but our marksmen are far in advance, on the horses.

We have now heavy timber ahead of us, and we suddenly hear the sound of approaching hoofs, and we halt. Our horsemen burst into view, with their horses on the run, and they breathlessly report, " Indians coming." The "scare" does not succeed well, and then Cowan informs us there is no water in advance for a distance of ten miles.

We turn back to the water, and select a suitable camping ground for the night. Arnold and myself go fishing, while the rest of the party get supper. We are soon summoned by Dingee's sonorous yell. The meal passed with no incident worthy of note. Oldham, in searching for a better seat on the grass, sat down upon some hot stewed peaches. He sprang to his feet, dropped his plate, grasped the seat of his breeches with both hands, looked heavenward, and payed emphatic tribute to his Maker by one single ejaculation, but there was none of this noteworthy, except it be his tragic pose, eloquent gestures and touching appeal. He was heartily applauded and, finding his plate, retired to the wagon tongue to rub his burn, and meditate on the possibility of iritating the saddle on the coming morrow.

Looking up the hill, we see pack animals coming. We suppose that it is Gen. Sherman's party coming from the geysers, and with no little interest hasten to get a better view of them. As they approach nearer we see that it is two mountaineers, who encamp below us.

Supper over, we washed dishes, built our camp fire, and brought out the musical instruments. Myers and Mann went to visit the mountaineers, and soon returned with them. We learned that they were old mountaineers, by the name of Wood and Hicks, and were prospecting, and had left Gen. Sherman's party two days before. We were disappointed to hear that Sherman had left the geysers, and returned by the way of Boseman, as we were expecting to meet him on our way. They told us that it would take us two days to reach the Park, as it would be necessary to cut our way through the woods. They bade us good night, and returned to their camp, while we went to sleep. No sound broke the stillness except the occasional yelp of the Cayote, as he views our camp fire.

August 14.—The nights are growing cool now, as we ascend the mountains, but it only makes sleep more refreshing and gives us better reason to respond with alacrity to Dingee's unearthly yell for breakfast. I start down the river to catch the horses, and as I pass the camp of the mountaineers, on my return, they salute me with the usual style of good bye, "so long ; good luck to you," and they strike off towards Lake Henry. This is, I believe, the last that was ever heard of these two men. They were probably caught by Chief Joseph's band, and it is my opinion that I saw Wood's mare with them subsequently.

We hitch up and take to the road again, for the Lower Geyser Basin. After rising the hill our road, for a distance of ten miles, lies through a densely timbered country. We again strike the Madison River, and camp for our noonday meal. Here the scenery is grand beyond description, as the river flows through mountains miles in height, and are as rough as rocks and timber can make them. We are now about three miles from the Upper Canyon, and, finding a desirable place to halt, stop for dinner.

A mile further on we come to vast quantities of fallen timber, and we find our progress impeded to such an extent that we are compelled to call our axes into requisition, and cut our way for more than a mile, when we again find open timber. (I wish to add that we shall present no claims against the government for building this road, as subsequently it gave Chief Joseph a better chance to get away from Gen. Howard, or *vice verce*.)

We drive down off the mountain to the river, which we find forks here, one branch coming from the north and the other from the east. Not knowing which of these to follow, we are evidently lost, but our apprehensions are soon relieved by a shout from Dingee, who has discovered the trail leading up the east fork. We follow it a short ways, and come suddenly to the mouth of the Canyon.

It is now but 3 P. M., yet we concluded to camp for the night, as we wish to make the passage of the Canyon earlier in the day.

At the supper which followed, consisting of game, fish, fruits, coffee and tea, Dingee again reminded us of his anticipated emaciation. It was noticeable that the fuller the fare the more he complained, and Oldham and myself were prompted to make a diagnosis of the case, and concluded that he either had the consumption or had formerly been used as a government store-house. The party concurring, the committee arose and we went to bed.

August 15.—The beautiful view that greets us in the bright sunlight of the early morning hastens our preparations to enter the canyon, and we are soon ready to cross the river, which we do immediately below our camp. The road follows the bank of the river, and a quarter of a mile from our place of crossing we enter the Upper Canyon of the Madison.

A mere pen description of the sublimity of this magnificent mountain passage way could convey no idea of its beauties. It is indescribably beautiful and grand. The poetry of nature seems to have collected here. We cross the river seven times in passing through it, although it is but six miles long, and come out on a large stream that flows from the north-east, which is called Gibben's Fork. Here we find a delightful place to camp, and halt for dinner. We find, also, that it is the site of the camp of Wood and Hicks on the night before we met them. We try fishing with good success, taking quite a number of white fish and trout, then cross the stream to the south bank. We now leave this stream, and begin the ascent of the divide that separates it from the Madison, which is now called the Fire Hole River.

The road since leaving camp this morning has been good, and along its borders we find raspberries and strawberries growing in abundance.

At half past three o'clock, we greet, with a hearty cheer, the appearance of the first geyser. It is a jet of steam thrown into the air three hundred feet, and is, apparently, about three or four miles from us. Two miles below us is plainly seen the Fire Hole River, and in a short time we reach it. Following up the river a mile, we come to an open flat where it forks, and we turn up the east fork some two hundred yards, and reach our first geyser or hot spring. It lies upon the other side of the river from us and we cross over to examine it more critically.

We found that it was a mound, composed of sedimentary deposit, about thirty feet in height, and the spring at its summit was about four feet in diameter. The water from the spring, ran sparkling down the side, forming a beautiful little rivulet, and thence flowing to the river.

We pause for a time to note its many beauties, then re-cross the stream to the wagons. We were now about three hundred yards from the timber, and at a point that afterwards was the scene of our capture by the Indians. But little did we think then, that subsequent events should indellibly impress upon us every feature of this, the place of our introduction into Wonder land.

We drive on up the east fork, about two hundred yards then cross, and are now surrounded by geysers and springs. The party scatter, each starting upon a tour of inspection without regard to the others. After a short ramble, I return to the buggy and drive on to the region of the Mud Pots, as they are called, which is but a few hundred yards in advance of where the party abandoned the wagons.

Tying the horses to a tree, I started upon a tour of observation. The "Mud Pots" or "vats," are just what the name indicates, a depression in the earth which is filled with a thick, grayish colored mud. The peculiarity of the pots or vats, is that the mud is in a constant state of ebullition, the ground about it giving forth a hollow, rumbling sound. They vary in diameter from four or five to ten feet, and the region in which they are found, covers an area of three or four acres. I was surprised to see no steam issuing from them, as I supposed they were intensely hot, but on putting my hand into the mud, I was more surprised to find that they were very cold. Sounding them, I found their depth to be from four to thirty feet.

I ascended a knoll near me, and on turning to the north, saw about a mile and a half distant, the Lower Geyser Basin. From this point I had an excellent view of the whole basin. Its many geysers, constantly spouting forth their columns of steam, gave it the appearance of a large manufacturing town.

Leaving the knoll and crossing to a ridge that lies on the right, I have an uninterrupted view of Fire Hole Basin. It is circular in form, and about a mile in diameter, with the Fire Hole River running through the center. The basin is filled with hot springs and small geysers, there being about a thousand within it, boiling and spouting from five to thirty feet.

From my position, I saw a number of our party on the banks of the river not far distant, and I descended and found that they were examining a hot spring in the edge of the river. It is thirty or forty feet in diameter, and the cold water of the river flows all about it. It is constantly pulsating, every four or five seconds, throwing a column of water ten to twenty feet in height, and at each pulsation it gives forth a pumping, rumbling sound. With no respect to his Satanic Majesty, and with no disrespect to this beautiful freak of nature, we call it the Devil's Tea Pot, because of its seeming appropriateness.

Immediately about this spring is a beautiful cascade about three feet in height, running clear across the river. The water falls in an unbroken sheet, presenting a beautiful appearance. It is about thirty feet above the Devil's Tea Pot. Here it was, that the E l of Dunraven caught a fine trout, and without moving from where he stood, turned and dipped it into the spring and cooked it upon the hook.

We now turn towards the ridge we have just crossed, and as we near its base, we discover a large spring, thirty feet in diameter, flowing from beneath it. It is more than beautiful, all the tints of the rainbow being reflected from its surface, blue predominating. We ascend the ridge and having regained its sumit, we pause for a time to view again, the wonders by which we are surrounded. As we are about to depart, we hear a call from Oldham, and proceeding in the direction of the sound, find him gazing into a large circular basin, forty or fifty feet in diameter, that is filled with boiling hot chalk. It is called a "chalk vat." It has the appearance of a vat of chalk or mortar, and keeps boiling away at a fearful rate. Leaving this vat, we go down a little ways, and find the Devil's Mud Pot, a vat filled with hot mud. It gives rise to the suggestion, that his Majesty has taken a contract to supply a wholesale establishment, with mud pies, and the way he flops and flirts it around gives credence to the belief that his reputation for close application to business is a merited one. I took a pole and pushed it into the mud in this vat about thirty feet, and it was slowly sucked beneath the surface, when suddenly, with a loud thump, it was thrown entirely out upon the surface, while the mud flies and splashes in every direction, spouting to the height of ten or fifteen feet. Discretion prompts us not to try the experiment again, and we returned to camp.

Myers and Mann have preceded us, and have supper in course of preparation when we arrive, and soon after Cowan and Dingee, who have been exploring on horse-back, join us. Each being anxious to recount his or her adventures and observations during the day, we agree to dicide by ballot who should first be entitled to the floor. After an unsucessful ballot, in which all got one vote, we agree to give Dingee the first chance, since he says he knows more about Satan than any of us. Just as he begins his narration, a flock of geese pass over us and alight not far distant. This promises roast goose, and all are interested in its flight, but none more so than Dingee. Cowan and Myers take their guns and follow them, and Dingee, listlessly resumes his narrative with his eyes scanning the heavens for another flock. He tells us that he and Cowan had visited the Lower Geyser Basin and—the cry of "grub pile," is wafted on the breeze, and with a bound and a cry of "next," he forfeits his honors and position as story teller for the evening and starts for his rations. While at supper we hear the reports of our hunters' guns, and soon after they return to camp, each having secured a large goose. After supper we indulge in our favorite evening diversion, and at ten o'clock all are asleep.

August 16.—At six o'clock, Dingee's dolorous yell awakes us to the indescribable beauties of our first morning in geyser land. The sun is shining brightly, and the air is perfectly calm. We despatch breakfast, and conclude to move our camp close up to the Spouting Geyser, and at eight o'clock we are on the move to the basin. We leave the east fork, and travel north-east a couple of miles and camp in a grove of pines about three hundred yards distant from Thud Geyser. This is a spouting geyser that throws a column of water about four feet in diameter, to a height of seventy-five or eighty feet, subsides, and again the immense column of water is ejected. It gets its name from the noise it makes as it ejects the water, something like "ca-thud." Its temperature is 185 degrees. We picketed our horses, each cut a serviceable walking stick, and start to visit the geysers.

We walk about a half a mile, and ascend a little mound where we see Fountain Geyser. This is a huge basin of one hundred and twenty-five feet in diameter, and a crater within the rim, of twenty-five feet in diameter. There is an elegantly carved rim around the outer crater three feet high, and during an eruption the representation of a beautiful fount, is most natural. Just now it is perfectly calm, and we again see the beautiful rainbow tints reflected from the surface. As the sun rises the tints change, and to the observer, it presents a beautiful appearance, indeed. We walk around it and view with unutterable pleasure, the reflected images of white clouds that are passing over head, that mingling, with the colors reflected from its surface, make it an object, upon the beauties of which, the eye never tires of resting.

As we look upon its calm surface, lying so innocently sparkling in the sun's rays, we cannot imagine that it will soon be spurting and charging as if a million demons were at work in its depths. As we look, a white bubble emerges from the large, dark hole at the bottom, rises to the surface and breaks. Another soon follows, then others in quick succession, and as they keep coming faster and faster, the water becomes agitated and in the middle of the spring begins to boil. It grows hotter and hotter, and in a few minutes comes out with a rushing noise, and spouts forty or fifty feet in the air, throwing its columns in different directions at each spout. It is now boiling and splashing at a fearful rate and the mind of one involuntarily reverts to the story of Satan and his imps, pounding, thumping and pumping brimstone with infernal ingenuity. Our party becomes enthusiastic over the wild grandure of the scene, and as each geyser "shoots off" in the air, like a rocket, with a roaring and "whishing" sound, we salute it with a demoniacal yell. The whole country becomes agitated, the earth trembles and heaves, the air is rent with hideous groanings and rumblings, and it seems as if all nature was going to destruction with infernal rapidity. It is terrible.

The eruption lasts for about an hour, when it seems the demons of power have become exhausted with their terrible throes, and sunk to rest. The water subsides, the surface is again calmer, and in a few minutes everything is perfectly still.

We now leave the Fountain Geyser, and ascend a mound that lies to the east a few hundred yards. From this we have an unobstructed view of the whole basin. Just below us, we see steam issuing from a basin with a "thump-lump" sound and on descending to investigate, we find an enormous chalk vat. It is filled with a boiling hot substance, resembling chalk, and its apance and smell of brimstone or magnesium, would naturally give rise to the remark of Arnold's, "It is where the devil mixes his mortar." Looking across the country to the other side of some timber, we see in the distance, probably a mile away, a geyser throwing a column of water and steam from one to two hundred feet high, we start to see it and on passing the timber, come out into another small basin in which we find many beautiful sulphur springs. They are of different colors, each having a tint peculiar to itself. In one, orange would predominate, in another sky blue, others would be dark red or green, and all were perfectly transparent. We gather some beautiful specimens here, then pass on a little ways to Dome Geyser.

This geyser has at one time, been one of considerable power, as the overflow has formed a mound fifteen feet in diameter; from its summit rises a chimney about eighteen feet in height, from the top of which steam issues constantly. Mr. Mann wished to sketch it and Myers and myself climbed to the top of it. From our position we could look down into its mouth, and could hear a rumbling sound in its depths. While we stood there the water, all of a sudden, and without any warning whatever, came spouting up above our heads. It may be presumed that we tumbled off in a hurry.

We continue on our course to the geyser we saw from the mound on the other side of the timber, and soon reach it. It is situated in the lower portion of this groupe, and from the fantastic architectural handiwork of nature here displayed, it is called Architectural Fountain Geyser. It has an elegantly scalloped circular basin about thirty feet in diameter at the base and twenty feet at the top or mouth, with vertical sides extending to an unknown depth. When we visited it, the water was calm, but was flowing over its rim, and thence to terraced pools, sparkling in the bright sunlight as it passed from one to the other and finally forming two little rivulets, on either side of the mound, and flowing away to the river.

We waited near this geyser most of the afternoon, expecting to see an eruption but were disappointed. The ladies, Cowan and Dingee, had returned to camp but the remainder of us lingered near it, carving our names on the side of the basin and searching for specimens. On the sides of the little basins surrounding the geyser, we found hundreds of names written with lead pencils. Some dated as far back as '66 and '67, and yet the names were as perfect as when written. Seeing a stone lying in the bottom of one of the basins. I bared my arm and took it out and found on one side of it the name "Miss Ella Aylesworth," written in lead pencil. I thought to rub the name off easily, but on trying to do so, found that it was indellible, and it was possible to remove it only with the blade of a knife.

As we were wandering around, each by himself, we heard a yell from Myers that was, seemingly, prompted by the acutest pain. Looking in the direction whence the agonizing cry came, we beheld Myers hopping towards us with one foot firmly clasped in his hands, and swearing terribly. Having reached us he began rolling and tumbling upon the ground, moaning, groaning and swearing as he writhed in contortions. As he struck a sitting posture we found he held his shoe in his hand. He pulled up his pants and began rolling down his stocking, and as he did so, the skin and flesh from the leg adhered to it. We then saw that he had stepped into a hot spring and that his limb was literally cooked. As the air struck the naked nerves, the pain must have been intense and again he writhed in agony. He grew calmer after a little, and ceased his rolling and swearing, when Arnold innocently asked "Was the spring hot?" There was an awful significance in the answer, "Yes,——you!"

Finding it impossible for him to return to camp in this condition, I told him that I would return to camp and send Dingee with a horse to meet him. I returned to camp, leaving Arnold with him, and dispatched Dingee with a horse and in about an hour they returned. Mann bandaged the leg as best he could and having made him as comfortable as we could, under the circumstances, we disposed of a hearty supper and, after the usual comparison of notes made during the day, retired.

August 17.—The usual dismal yawn of Dingee's awakes us at break of day, and just as we arise we hear Thud Geyser fire its morning salute. During breakfast we determined to go to the

Upper Geyser Basin, distant about ten miles, and shortly afterwards all are busy packing up. When about ready to leave, we are surprised by the appearance of three men and a boy who ride into camp. They prove to be Mr. Houston and party from Bear Gulch. He gives us the particulars of the Big Hole fight, the first that we had heard of it. He said that he did not apprehend any trouble from Indians, and as he and party are also *en route* for the Upper Basin, we determine to travel in company. We were glad of the acquisition to our party, as Mr. Houston is thoroughly conversant with every part of Geyserland, as he had visited it yearly for a number of years.

We soon reach the Fire Hole River which here flows from the east, and we follow up its course by a good trail two miles or more till we reach Devil's Half Acre, which lies on the other side of the river from us. Arnold and myself wade the stream and the party continue on up the river. We ascend an eminence two hundred feet high, perhaps, when a terrible rumbling sound tells us that we have reached the Devil's Half Acre and the Mammoth Hot Spring.

The Devil's Half Acre is thirty or forty feet square with walls of rock twenty or thirty feet high, surrounding it. It is horrible to stand on top of those walls and look down into the boiling, seething waters below, and one shudders and draws away at the first glimpse of the terrible commotion. It is certainly appropriately named.

Leaving this we visit the Mammoth Hot Spring, about one hundred and fifty yards away, and above. This we find as beautiful as the other is hideous. It is a basin shaped like an inverted saucer and three hundred feet in diameter at the top, and is the largest hot spring in the world. Its elevation is about fifty feet and the water is constantly flowing over the summit at all points, falling into little basins as it descends. Words are inadequate to convey the faintest idea of the beauties of this spring. The one just visited may justly be regarded as combining the horrors of a hell; in this is blended the beauties of a heaven. Looking into its depths we see the different rainbow tints, commencing with orange next the walls and ending in the center with dark blue. As the waters flow over the sides of the basin, the colors are yet more distinct and the line of separation is more distinctly disernable. First we notice the orange color which flows over a space of about ten feet, then passing around the basin we come to a space in which the waters are green, then follows red then blue and so on, each of the tints of the rainbow coming in regular succession. One never tires of its beauties. The different colors are not attributed to the position in which the rays of the sun strike the water, but rather to the minerals which the water contains, hence the colors are never changing.

We are loth to leave this most beautiful of the springs, but the advance of the party hastens our departure and we again passed up the river, seeing many springs as we go, to a point about two miles from where we crossed, and recross to the trail. Here we find Dingee and Oldham waiting for us with horses, and mounting, we soon overtake the party. We follow the left bank of the river for three miles and then the trail follows the base of the mountains by a zig-zag route for a distance of two miles when we again strike the river and after following up its course a mile we again leave it to our right and ascend the mountains on our left for a mile and a half when we come out on to the Upper Basin and the river again which we follow up two miles and cross the river, proceed up the stream a short distance and go into camp in a cluster of pines near Castle Geyser. This is a most desirable camping ground for a small party, as there is plenty of wood, shelter from the sun and rain, and hot and cold water within fifteen paces. Back of this camp about half a mile distant, there is an excellent pasturage for horses, consisting of a heavily grassed meadow of about two miles in circumference, in the middle of which is a large cold water spring.

We are now in Wonderland, and as we look around us and see the numerous geysers in full state of eruption, with others in quick succession throwing forth their vast columns of water, we realize that the Lower Basin is insignificant in comparison to this.

As we pitch our tents Mr. Houston points out the principal points of interest and as he is telling us of Old Faithful, a rumbling noise is heard, and he exclaims "Off she goes!" and a column of water one hundred and fifty feet high, is suddenly thrown into the air. We, with a shout, drop everything and make haste to see it, but on being told that an eruption will not take place again for sixty-five minutes we return to camp and prepare dinner. After dinner we, on consulting our watches, find that we have but ten minutes to walk the half mile that lies between us and Old Faithful and we make haste, as it is known that the entertainment is given at the exact moment advertised, with no postponement in deference to any thing.

We find a mound thirty or forty feet high, with little basins all around it which catch the water as it falls during an eruption. We pause, and hear beneath us a rumbling, rushing sound, and the water rises six or seven feet in the air and subsides a moment. Again it rises, still higher, and again subsides, each time seemingly gaining power until, with a roaring, rushing sound it sends a column of water five or six feet in diameter to a height of one hundred feet. The eruption continues for the space of fifteen or twenty minutes, being accompanied throughout, with its horrible groaning, then the water falls back into the little basins, and all is quiet again for the time.

We now visit in turn, the Giantess, that throws a column two hundred and sixty feet, the Bee Hive, with a spout of two hundred and nineteen feet by actual measurement, and two other smaller geysers called, respectively the Lion and Lioness, and then return to camp. Gathered about the camp fire during the evening, Houston gives us an elaborate discription of the wonders of this region, the half of which we have not seen, and relates many remarkable incidents that have taken place within its limits.

The party being tired they, with the exception of Arnold, Houston and myself, retire at nine o'clock, but we cross the river to see the eruption of the Grand Geyser by moonlight. We wait patiently until twelve o'clock but are disappointed and return to camp and "turn in."

About 3 A. M. we hear a yell, " Off she goes," and we jump to our feet at the warning sound of old Castle Geyser, which is about to belch forth his pent up wrath. We hear the premonitory rumbling and groaning, the earth jars and trembles with the mighty force below it; the noise becomes more distinct, and the throes of the earth more violent; in a moment a tremendous noise and roar like thunder follows, the earth gives a quick spasmodic quiver of agony, and a column of water twenty feet in diameter is thrown into the air one hundred feet high. For ten minutes it holds it in that position, when, having exhausted its fury, it drops back to the surface. With the same hollow, rumbling sound, a column of steam follows, shooting suddenly to a height of two hundred feet, and then gradually ascending to a distance of three hundred or four hundred feet, and rolling away with the upper air currents.

The moon is at the full, and as we are standing in the shadow of the jet of steam, we have one of the most strikingly beautiful views that ever the eye of man beheld. It seems like a solid column of silver. The steam soon passes away and soon again stillness reigns. We retire again, but not to sleep, and as we meditate upon the wonders of this more than wonderful region, we cannot but be reminded of the words of the psalmist, " What is man, that thou art mindful of him ? "

AUGUST 18.—A yell, not unlike an Indian war whoop, from Dingee, routes us out at 7 o'clock, and we are soon ready to do ample justice to our geyser coffee, potatoes boiled in the hot springs, and bacon. Dingee remarks that he has a " soft thing " of it now in the culinary department, as he does the cooking and dish-washing without fire.

We pass the day in wandering from point to point, inspecting the many wonders that are constantly found, each investigating for himself, and all intent on collecting specimens of rocks, minerals, vegetable growth, etc., and return to camp about 4 P. M.

Up to this time we have had the pleasantest weather imaginable, which is certainly surprising, since, owing to the moist climate and immense clouds of steam constantly arising, it can rain with as little preparation as any place in the world. As we came to camp, it had the appearance of rain, and, although the sun was shining brightly then, in ten minutes time it was pouring torrents. The pines, however, afford us an excellent protection, and after the rain ceases we dispose of supper, and carry the dishes to a spring for washing, which is done by throwing them into the water and poking them about with a stick for a few minutes, and remove them perfectly cleansed.

We had been expecting to witness an eruption of Grand Geyser, but, as yet, had been disappointed. After supper, while lying beneath a tree in camp, I saw, in the direction of this geyser, a column of water suddenly spout up some 30 feet high and then subside. With the shout, " There goes the Grand Geyser," we start pell-mell to see it. We cross the river on a run, and proceed some five hundred yards towards the mountain ere it is reached.

This is Hayden's favorite geyser, and, as regards beauty and nice fountain work, it is far superior to anything in Geyser Land. Houston says that it has changed in the last few years, and does better work now than it ever did before. As we approach it " goes off " again, spouting forty or fifty feet high, then subsiding. Again it spouts, and again subsides. Again and again it throws up its immense column that is five or six feet in diameter, and in the space of thirty minutes it has made nine eruptions, each coming with greater power and spouting higher than that which preceded it, until finally, with a mighty roar, it throws its column of water one hundred and twenty-five feet high. It holds it in that position for five or eight minutes, then drops back again to its basin. This geyser differs from the others in the manner of its eruption, and in the fact of its having so many eruptions in such a short space of time lies its beauty and popularity.

As the water recedes, we step to view the crater, and see nothing but a large hole in the earth with sides sloping to the center.

Mr. Cowan and Oldham step down into it and commence carving their names, when suddenly, without warning, the water rises beneath them. It may be imagined that they did not stop to finish their carving. The water fills the basin and then becomes calm.

We return to camp and witness an eruption of Steam Geyser, but as this is constantly at work, and not far distant, it soon loses its novelty. It is continually giving off its thumping, pumping sound, and we soon wish that it would take a rest, or give us one. Night and day we hear that same monotonous thumping.

In camp we prevail upon Mr. Houston to relate some of his experience in the Rocky Mountains, which are full of interest and romance. We retire to lay awake listening to the unearthly sounds that we hear all around us rather than to rest.

AUGUST 19.—This is Sunday, the day of rest, but nature here does not heed it and keeps up her gratuitous exhibitions without intermission. We soon tire of lying around camp and again sally forth on a tour of discovery. We return shortly and conclude that we will do our washing since such an opportunity for "boiling clothes" will not be presented again soon. Emma and Ida put their clothes in a pillow case, Dingee took off his blouse and tied a large stone in it and I finished tying it with my handkerchief; Arnold also removed his jacket and we repaired to the laundry, Old Faithful. We hear the preparatory rumbling and the waters rise a few feet above the surface. Mr. Houston now gives the command to cast them into the water. It goes down and remains so long that we begin to feel uneasy, and Dingee begins to lament his loss and to bless the man who "put the job up" on us. Mr. Houston remarks that it will be all right, and the next instant, with a rush and a roar she "goes off" and the clothes, jacket, rags, &c., mixed in every conceivable shape, shoot up to a distance of a hundred feet or more and fall with a splash in the basins below. The water subsides, and we fish out the clothing which we find as nice and clean as a Chinaman could wash it with a week's scrubbing. Dingee rejoiceth.

4

Wishing to experiment, we collect an immense quantity of rubbish and drop it into the crater. We have filled it to the top with at least a thousand pounds of stones, trees, stumps, &c., and now sit down to await further developments. At the exact time advertised, sixty-five minutes from the time of the last eruption, the earth begins to tremble, we hear the rush again, "off she goes," and away go rocks, trees and rubbish to a height of seventy-five or eighty feet in the air. Old Faithful seems to have been angered by such an unwarrantable proceedure on our parts, or wishes to show us how frutile are our attempts to check his power and furnishes an entertainment of unusual magnitude and duration.

We find many curious specimens of petrifaction here, and it seems that any article frequently immersed in these waters soon becomes petrified. Ida finds a petrified handkerchief that is perfectly white, and every thread of which is distinctly visible. Mann finds two more imbedded in the rocks, and cuts them out. Mr. Cowan finds a petrified mouse, and Mr. Oldham finds a nice specimen of writing paper and part of an envelope, and a rabbit's ear, and others find many very remarkable curiosities.

We next visit the Giantess, which is said to be the finest geyser in the basin. It has a crater twenty by twenty-five feet, and throws a column of water two hundred and sixty feet in height. We did not witness an eruption of this geyser; we could see a great hole in the earth, some seventy-five or eighty feet deep, filled to the brim with clear hot water, at the bottom of which we could see a dark cavern from which 'the water rushes during an eruption, which latter usually lasts from six to twelve hours. An eruption from this one geyser is well worth weeks of waiting to witness.

We visit the Bee Hive Geyser and witness an eruption, and the party now separates. Dingee, one of Houston's party. named Sterling Henderson, and myself, start for a place upon the mountain back of the Giantess, whence we see steam issuing above the tree tops. We ascend the mountain some one thousand feet above the level of the basin, and find a large hot spring about seventy-five feet in diameter, the waters of which are boiling away at a fearful rate.

There is no evidence that this spring spouts, but it is constantly overflowing, and the water, as it runs down the mountain side, kills everything with which it comes in contact. There is a sedimentary deposit, that it has made from time to time, in its different paths, that is about three hundred yards wide and five or six hundred yards long. The water does not cover this area, but is confined to a narrow channel five or six feet wide, which it fills to the depth of two or three inches. The channel must be constantly shifting, the water seeking a new outlet as each channel is filled. The sides and bottom of this little stream are of varied colors, owing to the presence of mineral substances, and are very beautiful.

We sit down to gaze for a time on its wondrous beauties, but are aroused by a prolonged shout in the distance. Dingee exclaims: "There goes Giant Geyser!" and a look in the direction indicated verifies the statement. It is two miles distant, but we bound away on the run. We soon reach it, and find the old fellow tearing away at a fearful rate. The rest of the party have beaten us there, and we find them sitting beneath the trees watching the fearful convulsions of this more than grand geyser. Words are inadequete to give but a tithe of its grandeur. It is indescribably awful. The eruption continued about two hours.

We next visited Grotto Geyser, situated on a mound of pure white silica, and encircled by a cluster of hot springs. Its unique formation must be seen to be appreciated.

After supper we again visit Old Faithful and witness another eruption, then return to camp; see Grand Geyser in full play, and tired of the repetitions of the wonders of the day, we soon are sound asleep, totally obvious to the terrors by which we were surrounded or the surprises held in store for us.

AUGUST 20.—At nine o'clock Houston informed us that he and party were going back by the way of Yellowstone Lake and Falls and wishes to know if any of our party wants to accompany him. Arnold, Dingee and myself conclude to visit the lake, distant forty-five miles, and then return to the Lower Geyser Basin and rejoin the party, which would remain there for us. We are soon in the saddle and at ten o'clock bid the party good bye and are off. Just as we leave camp old Castle Geyser fires a farewell salute, and as we pass the Grotto, Riverside and others we see them doing excellent work, worthy an aspirant to political honors.

As we reach the point where the Mammoth spring lies immediately opposite us, we cross the river and take a last view of this remarkable body of water. We linger for a time loth to leave, then resume our way down the river, which we recross, and at one P. M. are at our camp in the Lower Basin.

Here we find Mr. Cowan's dog Dido, which we had left on shifting our camp to the Upper Basin. For a time she disputed our entrance into camp, but on recognizing Cowan's horse which I was riding, she concluded that matters were all right and permitted us to enter. The faithful brute was almost starved as we had left nothing for her to eat and she had been without food since Friday.

We prepare dinner and Dingee lays in provisions for a four days' trip. At 2:30, we are again on the road, taking the dog with us.

We leave the Lower Basin by the Bozeman route, and travel up the east fork of the Fire Hole River, seeing numerous extinct geysers and sulphur springs on either side of the trail. We follow the course of the stream for a distance of ten miles, when we reach the foot of the mountains separating the valley of the east fork of Fire Hole River from that of the Yellowstone.

As we begin the ascent of the mountains, an old man suddenly steps from the bushes into the trail before us. He was the most wretched looking specimen of humanity I had ever seen. Mr. Houston grasped his gun, and the stranger saluted us in a friendly way and drew near. He told us that his name was John Shiveley, direct from the Black Hills. He gave us a mountaineer's account of his travels and concluded by asking Mr.

Houston if we had any spare provisions. Houston's party did not have any, but Arnold told him that our camp was at Tower Basin, where he would find an abundance of "grub" and that he could help himself. He did not tarry long, and receiving directions from us as to the right trail, passed on.

We continued the ascent of the mountains. We cross them soon and complete the descent by night fall and camp on a little creek, called Warm Spring Creek. We picket the horses, dispose of supper, and after the usual talk till eleven o'clock, turn in, satisfied with the day's travel of thirty-five miles.

AUGUST 21.—We arise to an early breakfast and bestir ourselves for the day's journey. While we are making preparations, Arnold takes his hook and tries to fish for trout in the stream upon which we are encamped. He succeeds in taking but a half dozen small ones. They are smaller than the common mountain trout and have small red spots upon their sides. Mr. Houston says that this is the only place in the mountains where this species of fish is caught. They cannot get down this stream as there are boiling hot springs in this stream, one half mile below, and neither can any others get to them. We found that they were of excellent flavor.

Soon after breakfast we again take to the saddle and strike out on a swinging gallop for the Yellowstone Lake, ten miles distant. Three or four miles from camp we suddenly come upon a party from Bozeman. It proves to be Storey and Riche's party, consisting of five men with guide, and four pack animals. We learn that they are *en route* for the geysers, where we tell them they will find our party, and with the usual mountain salutation "so long," we pass on. Three miles brings us to the summit of a rise from which we have our first view of the Yellowstone River. We can see it winding to the north for five or six miles and from our position it looks like a river of silver. Its nearest point is but a quarter of a mile below us, and we are soon upon its banks. To the left of us we see a mud geyser, and it being not far distant, we visit it for the purpose of investigation.

We find that the basin is circular in form, and about sixty feet in diameter. It is filled with boiling hot mud and in an eruption goes through the same process as a water geyser but frequently with more astonishing effects upon the beholder, as the mud flies in every direction, and should a particle touch the skin the sensation is the same as produced by dropping burning sealing-wax upon it.

We pass around this geyser to the left and Mr. Houston points out the location of the Devil's Well, which we set out to visit.

It is upon the side of the mountain, one hundred and fifty feet above the trail, and an examination reveals an enormous hole in the ground about twenty feet in diameter and forty feet deep, with perpendicular walls. Steam is constantly issuing from its mouth, but as it is blown aside for an instant, we see the boiling, seething waters at the bottom. They are surging and rushing at a fearful rate, and reminds one of the splashing waters of the "tail-race" of a mill. The steam arises in puffs, like that from an engine, and we hear, in the depths, horrible clinking and clanking, as if the devil was busily employed in manufacturing chains. The well is certainly correctly named.

Just below us we visit and inspect with no little curiosity a number of Arsenic Springs. Everything about them is covered with a slimy green substance, that gives it a very disagreeable appearance. We did not loiter here, as the steam arising from the waters is sickening, and very poisonous. We remount, return to the river bank, and take the trail leading to the lake, distant six miles south, up the river.

As we are pushing ahead at a brisk canter, we suddenly meet a mountaineer, who is driving a number of loose horses. We stop, and Houston advances and makes inquiry as to who he is and where bound. The man gives a satisfactory account of himself and passes on. Shortly afterward another man emerges from the bushes ahead. He is a tall, powerfully built man, and as he rode carelessly along, with his long rifle crossed in front of him, he was a picture. He was dressed in a complete suit of buckskin, and wore a flaming red neckerchief, a broad *sombrero*, fastened up on one side with a large eagle feather, and a pair of beautifully beaded moccasins. The costume of the man, his self-confident pose, and the quick penetrating glance of his keen black eye, would give the impression that he was no ordinary mountaineer. We meet; Houston recognizes him, it is the world renowned Rocky Mountain hunter and scout, Texas Jack. While Houston was in conversation with him, our party sat silently staring at him. This is our first sight of the man, whom, above all others, we were anxious to see, and we were in a measure excusable for our seeming impertinence. He inquired for "spare grub;" we had none to give him or sell, but told him that Storey and Riche's party were but a little ways ahead of him, and he could be provided for by them. He bade us good-day and pushed ahead.

We again struck a canter, and half a mile further on encountered two more men, both of whom were dressed in buck-skins and wore large *sombreroes*. They told us that they were Englishmen, traveling through the United States for pleasure and adventure, and that they, with Texas Jack as guide, had come through the mountains from Cheyenne to Yellowstone Lake for the purpose of fishing and hunting. They were now *en route* for the geysers, and on telling them that they would meet our party there, who would supply them with provisions, continued on their road.

We now left the river, which turns abruptly to the left, and began the ascent of the mountains. Two and a half miles further on we reach the summit, and pause to feast our eyes on as pretty a scene as mortal ever beheld. A thousand feet below us, stretching away to the south thirty miles, lie the placid waters of Yellowstone Lake. It is so calm that it looks like a huge mirror surrounded by verdure-covered mountains, that tower thousands of feet above it. Words cannot tell of the loveliness of the scene. Mr. Houston says that although he has visited it every year for ten years, he never fails to stop where we now are and drink in the beautiful view. We linger for some time, and note the many points of beauty, and watch the hundreds of water-fowl floating upon its surface, then, at the call of our guide, we begin the descent. About two hundred feet above the level of the lake, we find a nice camping place in a grove of small pines, where there is wood and cold spring water in abundance.

Supper is soon ready and the familiar cry of "grub pile" was never sweeter, and it may be remarked with all truthfulness, that it was the only thing *sweet* about the supper. Dingee, with his morbid dread of "loosing that twenty pounds," is usually the first to respond, and this occasion was not an exception. He drops on the grass, lunges for the bread, takes a bite, spits it out, and throws his whole soul into one prolonged sulphureous oath. We are astonished, and, through the force of habit acquired in the basins, draw back in expectation of an eruption by Dingee. Just as each has his mouth in proper position for exclaiming "there she goes," which we could each see formed upon the lips of the others, Dingee's breath gives out and he is of necessity, compelled to stop swearing. Arnold plays a good second as he takes a bite, and I investigate a mouthful. *It is two thirds salt.* Dingee indignantly asks if I had put all the salt into the flour sack, and I plead guilty to one cup only. I explained further that I had put in four cups of sugar to sweeten it, and light begins to dawn when I learn that the sugar was taken from another salt sack. Arnold materially assists our investigations by saying that *he* had put in two more cups of sugar from that same sack, making in all, six pints of salt to eighteen pounds of flour. The presence of the milk in the coacoanut is thus fully acounted for.

It is, perhaps, unnecessary to state that no one cares for bread at dinner, and immediately after, we make arrangements with Houston for exchanging salt for flour, with fair results.

The whole party are soon collected on the beach below camp, and start for a stroll. Arnold, who, it has probably been noted, is the Izaak Walton of the party, goes fishing, and the remainder of us gather specimens of the stones and petrified wood. Dingee and myself collect an immense quantity of rubbish, but had we known that it would all go to enrich Chief Joseph's cabinet, we certainly would not have lugged them so far. That statement may be relied upon as fact.

We follow the beach, which is about thirty yards wide and passes clear around the lake, to a point about three miles from where we struck it. We find an old log house, and near it a sailboat turned bottom upwards. The owner of both had gone to the Black Hills and left everything. We found tools with which to repair the boat, but concluded that it would be of no avail, as we were expecting to remain but a little while. While we were inspecting the premises, one of the party had found, in a slough near by, a row boat which we carried to the lake and launched. Three of us manned it, and pulled out for deep water.

We had our fishing tackle along, and it was no little amusement to catch the large salmon trout, with which the lake abounds. Our bait was grasshoppers, and as it touched the water a salmon would bound out of the water, seize it, and the way he would go until brought up by the end of the line. Then follow the trolling to get it into the boat. It is exquisite sport. We caught many that were eighteen or twenty inches long, and would weigh nine or ten pounds.

Houston points out the many points of interest, and gives a graphic description of the noteworthy objects that surround us.

At the south end of the lake we see Mount Evarts, the place where Evarts became separated from his party and got lost. It is said that he wandered for thirty days with little or no food, and was finally picked up on the other side of the lake. Looking to the east we see in the distance, probably forty or fifty miles away, the Old Man of the Mountain. It is a mountain in the shape of a human face, turned towards the sky. It is as perfect as if chiseled.

The profile of this wonderful image as seen against the horizon, is formed by the configuration of a chain of mountains, and being assured that we could see more of the outline from the mountains back of the log house, turn and are soon at the point indicated. Looking east we can see the whole outline of the form, and it is truly a remarkable image. The body, face and limbs, with knees slightly bent, and feet, are very distinctly portrayed. It is well worth going to see and no tourist that visits this lake should go

5

away without beholding it. Where we stand is the best point for observation.

We return to our camp and Houston points out Steamboat Spring, which stands on the north-east shore of the lake about twelve miles distant. It is so called from the noise it makes during an eruption, which is not unlike the whistle of a steamboat. We heard it the following morning and it sounded to me like a bugle call in the distance. We would liked very much to have visited it, but having no means of transportation across the lake other than a small, leaky boat, and it not being easily accessible by land, we were compelled to forego the pleasure.

On this side of the spring is a place called Specimen Beach, where there are found many curious petrifactions, such as fish, shells, wood, etc., but we cannot visit them.

Shortly after we return to camp, or at about five o'clock, a ripple is seen upon the lake and the wind springs up from the south-east. Houston remarks that we would soon witness a scene that would be grand in the extreme. The wind continues to rise and in a little time the whole lake is lashed into the wildest fury. We go down to the beach and spend some time in watching the "white caps," rolling towards us. The pelicans, swans and gulls come sailing towards us on the crest of the waves, and come within thirty or forty yards of the shore, then rising from the crest of a wave, sail away with a shrill cry that, mingling with the roar of the wind and waves, makes one's blood curdle.

As we stood here watching the commingling of the raging elements, we silently returned thanks that an all-wise Providence had prevented our launching the frail sail-boat, as it now would have been bottom upwards in the waters of the lake, with us beneath it, if Dingee had insisted on another exhibition of his seaman-like qualities.

Soon we hear the soft voice of Dingee sweetly warbling above the howling of the storm, "grub pile" and we return to camp. We had neglected to picket our horses, and after supper start in search of them. We searched until ten o'clock without finding them and returned to camp convinced that they had been stampeded, or stolen. We had nothing but a pack mule left us, and he, poor fellow, was anxious to go also, and all night long kept up his tramp, tramp at the end of his lariat and would frequently give vent to his longings by a prolonged bray.

Reaching camp Dingee sat down and began to dismally bewail his hard luck. We tried to console him with the assurance that he would now have an opportunity to walk off that superfluous amount of flesh and thus fulfill his prophecy of losing twenty pounds, but he refused to be comforted. We sadly turn in, and all is quiet for a time, when a voice breaks the stillness with "A Starry Night for a Ramble," while Dingee growls and the mule brays.

AUGUST 22.—At daylight the party were up and went in search of the horses. I remain in camp and relieve Dingee in the *cuisine*. In the course of time I have a frugal repast prepared and spread upon the ground. I gave the prolonged howl that usually brings us to meals, and as the call penetrates the valleys and is reverberated from hill to hill, an indistinct answer is heard afar off down the lake shore. Again I call, and again comes the answer, "nearer, clearer than before." It is Dingee, who, with the rest of the party some distance in the rear, soon come hastily into camp, but without the horses. The whole party were sullen, and we sit down to our meal in no enviable frame of mind. A prospective tramp of thirty-five miles, over the rugged mountain is not cheering. The name of the Creator was pronounced, but not in grace, as they contemplated the scanty fare. "A short horse is soon curried" may in a measure be given as one reason for the hastily despatched meal, but I attributed it to the fact of the entire absence of horse.

We silently consider for a time, the undesirable state of affairs then consult together. We have an alternative. It is either to walk or take the little boat and go down the Yellowstone to the point at which we struck it as we came. Neither suits Houston and he proposes another hunt for the horses. We separate and scour the woods in every direction, but with no better result than before.

Returning to camp I proposed to Houston that we turn the mule loose, believing that it could find the horses, if it had but one eye. Houston acting upon the idea, jumped upon its back and gave it the lariat. It immediately struck for the timber, and took a bee line for two and a half miles and walked in among the horses. In the course of half an hour Houston returns and we give a yell that shakes the hills and causes the dry boughs in the forest to fall in a copious shower. Dingee cries with joy and it is with the utmost difficulty that we restrain him from embracing the mule. I allay his exuberance of spirits by promising him my share of dinner.

We are soon ready for our departure and take a lingering look at the lake. The storm has ceased, and it now lies as calm as if nothing had ever caused a ripple upon its surface. The most vivid imagination would fail to portray its beauties.

We turn mountainward and retrace the course that we came. At the summit we stop and take the last long gaze at the Yellowstone Lake, the finest scene in the Rocky Mountains. We start our horses on a canter and are soon at the Mud Spring and Devil's Well again. These we pass without stopping, and push onward towards the Yellowstone Falls.

Five miles further down the river, we come to Sulphur Mountain, which we stop for a time to examine. It is about one thousand feet high, and fully four miles in circumference at the base, and receives its name from the amount of sulphur found in the minerals of which it is principally composed. The summit is composed of soil, upon which a few stunted pine trees grow, but the base and sides are composed of almost pure sulphur, the percentage being about eighty. We find the sulphur in the form of crystals, resembling honey-comb more than anything else, and are very pretty. It is hot, and I am convinced (not by any experiments made in person, however,) that it will cure any case of seven-year itch known, even if it has attained its majority: that is of three terms standing. On the west side of the base of the mountain, there is a hot boiling spring about twenty-five feet long by ten feet wide. It was quiet, and the surface had a phos--

phorescent appearance, which suggested the remark that if the devil should dip one of his victims in its waters and set him on fire, he certainly would burn forever.

Close to this is another sulphur spring that is pumping and threshing away industriously. The smoke and steam arising from this emits a fearful stench, and we do not care to get too close. Here we gather some nice crystals and remount. Houston remarks that Satan owns this country, and advises us to make peace with his Majesty; at least temporarily. Our observation here convinces us that if Moody and Sankey could bring this mountain, with its springs, and their congregations in juxtaposition, their labor would be greatly decreased and their converts millions.

As we leave the mountain we, at a little distance from it, cross Alum Creek, a small stream flowing from the west. Houston says that near its head there is a spring, the waters of which are strongly impregnated with alum. He says a mouthful of the creek water will pucker one's mouth so that it will be impossible for him ever to attain the accomplishments of a third-class whistler. We were perfectly willing to take his word for it, and did not experiment.

Five miles beyond this we approach the Yellowstone Falls, the roaring of which we hear before we get near them. The noise grows louder as we advance, and shortly we strike the river at the first rapids, about two hundred feet above the Upper Fall. Here we find that the trail divides, one turning to the left, which is the Bozeman trail, and the other following the river. Taking the right hand trail, we cross a creek, then ascend a steep mountain about five hundred yards, and camp beneath the wide spreading branches of a large spruce pine. It is now three o'clock, and we unsaddle, and proceed to get dinner. Dingee discovers a notice posted on the tree, which he reads for *our* benefit. It reads as follows:

Tourists are requested not to break, destroy or take away any specimens, under a penalty of fifty dollars fine, or one year in the penitentiary. By order of the Superintendent of the Na-

tional Park. We tell Dingee to make a memorandum of it, and he quietly observes that I can make up my mind for a year's sojourn in the penitentiary. We sit down to grub, but you can rest assured that our horses are securely picketed first.

Dinner over we start to view the falls. We ascend the mountain a little farther, then turn to the right some two hundred yards, and get our first glimpse of the Lower Falls of the Yellowstone. We are now fully three thousand feet above the falls, and from our position the scenery is indescribably grand. The river winding through the canyon below us looks like a shining thread of silver, as it glistens in the sun. It seems that one could step across it, and we can hardly credit the statement of Houston when he informs us that it is over one hundred feet wide. At this point we have the finest view of the canyon that it is possible to obtain, and to me, there is no better point from which to view the falls. We are standing above, and are looking distinctly down upon them. The water above is dashed into a turbulent, foamy cascade, by its ragged bed and lightning speed, but just at the edge of the fall it becomes smooth, as if pausing in awe at the dizying height from which it must spring, then leaps perpendicularly *three hundred and ninety feet* to its narrow bed below. Down the river, as far as the eye can reach, there rises, to the height of two thousand feet above the river, a grand, vast wall, so gorgeously colored and tinted that no painting or description can ever do it justice. Such is the force of the descent that the water, ere it reaches the rocky bed below, is dissolved into spray, and a cloud of it hangs constantly beneath the precipice. As the evening sun strikes this we see a perfectly formed rainbow. It is gorgeously beautiful.

We sit here for at least an hour, and when we rise to return to camp Houston tells us that he and party are going to Clark's Fork. We go back to camp, and bid them good bye, and at five o'clock they are off.

Arnold, Dingee and myself, now start for the Upper Falls, about a half mile, or perhaps less, above us. These falls will not bear comparison with the Lower Falls, but they are, nevertheless, strikingly beautiful. The water above flows calmly till within a few hundred feet of the falls, when it suddenly breaks, is lashed in a fury, and rushes headlong, as if bent upon destruction, and leaps outward over the precipice. It falls one hundred and eighty feet. Dingee proposes that we descend to the foot of the fall, and by dint of hard work, clinging to the jagged rocks and crevices, with fingers and toes, we make the descent. Here we have a finer view than from above, and the setting sun greatly exhances the beauty of the scene.

As we sit watching the water as it strikes in the bed, we see many large trout vainly endeavoring to ascend the cataract. They will spring six or eight feet up the sheet of water and drop back, then try it again with the same result. They seemingly never learn by their failures nor tire of their futile efforts. We sat and watched them some time, when I asked Dingee if he thought they would get up. He said they might if we would but give them time. I proposed that we shut off the water and help them up, but he said he thought we had better not as it might detain us—beyond supper time.

Night was drawing near and we thought to return, but discovered that scaling the precipice was another thing to going down it. We descended with the utmost difficulty, although it could have been more easily accomplished by falling, if not as satisfactory. But although we understand how the vigilanters used to instruct persons in falling up, we were loth to assist each other in that way.

We turn down the canyon to a point about three hundred yards below where we come to the little creek that we crossed just before going into camp. Here, after an immense amount of climbing and clinging, scratching and swearing, we succeed in reaching the creek whence we ascended to the brink of the canyon. We returned to the Lower Falls and concluded to descend into the canyon from the height above. It was with no little difficulty that we accomplished the feat, and we were well repaid for the trouble. Never did mortal eye behold a sight of more sublime magnificence than is afforded us as we cautiously peer into the abyss from the very brink of this majestic cliff. On the verge of the precipice we found a small pine tree growing, and notwithstanding the Superintendent's notice, we could not refrain from leaving our names upon it. One of the party posted a notice upon the tree which we have no doubt will be conformed to, not only more strictly, but more agreeably. It read thus:

Notice: Tourists are requested not to jump over these falls, as it spoils the fishing below. By order of the Superintendent.

We scale the mountain, return to camp, repicket our horses, build the camp fires for the night, and are soon recuperating from the fatigues of the day in sound sleep.

AUGUST 23.—We pass an uncomfortable night, owing to the cold, and daylight reveals the fact of it being an exceedingly restless one, too, as we find that by our efforts to keep warm we have tumbled and rolled about fifteen feet from where we laid down. We collect wood for the camp fire, and, having thawed out, prepare our frugal repast, which consists, principally, of salt bread. We are soon *en route* for the Lower Geyser Basin and home. The air is very pure and invigorating, and as we strike a mile or so of good trail, we give our horses the rein, and, with a war whoop, strike out at a spanking rate.

After riding four or five miles we come back again towards Alum Creek. When within about a mile of the creek, we find another trail leading off to the west or southwest, and, as this is the trail that Houston told us to take on our back route, we follow it for about two miles and come out on the creek near the side of a mountain with scrubby pines on the side and summit. This, in view of subsequent events, is an important landmark.

We follow the south fork of this stream some ten miles and come to Alum Spring. Its clear cold water is very inviting to the thirsty, but as Houston had told us of its peculiarities, we were not thirsty enough to drink.

As Houston was coming to the geyser, he told the boy, Henderson, that this spring was the last cool water he would find for some time, whereupon the boy dismounted and took a huge mouthful and—spit it out without being told to do so. By the time he could get the pucker out of his mouth, and find words to express the pent up anguish of his soul, his wrath had fled and Houston thus escaped the most complete errudiate and accomplished cussing of his life. A little water with something in it, be it heat or mineral, contains a great deal of latent eloquence.

We ascend the mountain separating Geyser Land from the Yellowstone, and find we are on a different trail from that which we passed over on Monday. This one leads down the mountain by way of Mary's Lake. As we proceed we come to more sulphur springs, where we gather more specimens of crystalized sulphur for Chief Joseph's cabinet. A mile or so beyond we come out on Mary's Lake which we find, is a beautiful sheet of water a half mile long, by one fourth of a mile in width, situated upon the summit of the divide. We water our horses, gather some specimens of the rock formation, pass along the western shore and soon begin the descent of the mountain, to the Lower Geyser Basin. The trail now runs almost perpendicularly up and down the mountains, and it is next to impossible to sit on our horses. I do not meet with such difficulty as the others, inasmuch as the long ears of my charger prevent my slipping over his head. Eight miles of this route brings us to the foot of the mountain where we again meet Texas Jack and party going back toward Yellowstone Falls. We chat for a time and he informs us that we will meet Riche's party coming up.

On the marsh, at the base of the mountain the trail is very indistinct and it is with difficulty that we find it. By keeping to the left, however, we find it and come out upon our trail of Monday at the place where we met the old man Shrively. We had not met Riche's party and conclude that they have taken the other trail to the falls. The marsh which we had just left was covered with hot springs, mud, willows and tall grass and to this fact may be attributed my ability to write this book. Had it not been for the willows and high grass it might have been otherwise, upon the principle that "dead men tell no tales." This will become manifest as the reader progresses. A mile

GIANT GEYSER, 200 FEET HIGH.
Page 35.

farther down we come to Texas Jack's dinner camp, and it being now two P. M., we conclude to camp here. We picket horses, build camp fire and are about to dine off the scanty provisions we have left, when Dingee announces with a cry of gladness that he has found the hind quarters of an eagle that Texas Jack or some of his party had killed a few hours before. Dingee seems to think that it is quite an acquisition to our depleted larder, and immediately sets about preparing it for dinner. He fries the legs, and the usual summons to "grub" is given with an amendment, "and eagle bird by chance." Perhaps the old pioneers of Virginia, M. T., will appreciate the amendment, when they remember Saxy, of Virginia, in the gem where he kept his roulette table, in '64. As he gave the wheel a turn, with the exclamation! "houchy, couchy, couchy, couchy; ninety-nine in the red, or eagle bird by chance!" I remember it distinctly, as having invested five dollars in the game, my father forcibly impressed it upon my mind, and elsewhere with a shingle.

As we sit down, we again hear the " eagle bird by chance," as Dingee lays hold of a leg with his teeth, but fails to fetch any meat. I pass my share out to the dog, Dido. It may be noted that our dinner of the next day was taken at the same place as was this, but with a largely increased number, and much less hilarity. We, also, had " bird by chance," but it was White Bird.

Dinner over, we, in a spirit of fun that will, at times, move the most sedate, decorate ourselves and horses with the eagle feathers in true Indian style, and, remounting our horses, give the Indian war whoop and strike out on a gallop for the home camp in the basin. For three miles down the east fork of the Fire Hole River, our trail is good, but on crossing we find the trail is through fallen timber, which necessitates slower traveling. In passing through the timber three miles, we cross the east fork three times, but we finally come out on the east side of the stream. Off to the right we hear a gun fired, and presently see a man running towards us. He comes to the opposite bank of the stream, when we see that it is old man Shrively. He says he has lost his horses; had traced them this far, and inquires if we have seen them. Being answered in the negative, he asks if we will carry his " traps " to the settlement, in case he does not find his horses, and we consent. Subsequent events show that this arrangement was unnecessary as Chief Joseph kindly relieved us of the necessity of looking after them. In that way his magnanimity is overpowering.

We ask the old man to come to our camp and stay over night, and push onward leaving him to continue his search.

An hour's ride brings us near camp, when putting the spurs to our horses we give the war whoop and rush headlong into camp. We are greeted by all the party with a cordial "How, how," and in me, Oldham recognizes a long lost chief, Red Eagle, but Dingee dispels the illusion by asserting that " we are the lost babes of whoop-up-or-any-other-man."

As we dismount, Dingee imploringly asks for cold victuals and *unsalted* bread. Mrs. Cowan, assisted by the others, soon prepares an excellent repast and Dingee proceeds to make amends for the days of fasting, while I relate our adventures. The account of our adventures were not without tints, and it is a small estimate to say that the amount of provisions consumed by Dingee was fully in proportion to the amount of coloring used by me.

We find the party in excellent spirits and Myers, although yet a cripple, hobbles around with good grace.

There is another party in camp by the name of Harmon, a prospector from Colorado, whom we had met in Riche's party, and we were told that old man Shrively had taken breakfast with them in the morning and had lost his horses while eating breakfast in their camp.

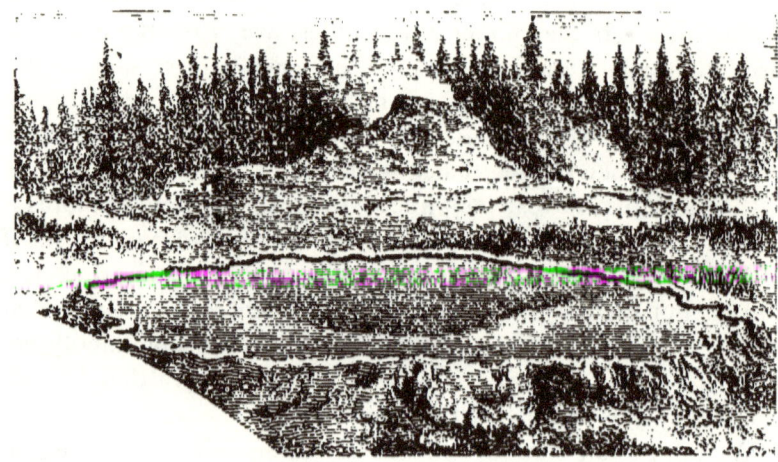

CASTLE GEYSER—PAGE 31.

It is now seven o'clock, and we build an enormous camp fire and call a council to decide our future wanderings. The result of the conference is, that, having seen the sights, we will start for home in the morning.

This being our last night in the Basin we institute a grand jollification. The guitar and violin are produced and music, singing, and dancing follows. Mann makes a sketch of the camp, with Oldham conspicuous in his Indian costume, in which we have dressed him for the occasion. We finish the evening's entertainment with a "pigeon wing" from Dingee, a "double shuffle" from Arnold, and a song in full chorus, entitled "Flitting Away."

The events that follow have vividly impressed upon the minds of all, the closing lines of the song:

"Flitting, flitting away,
All that we cherish most dear."

We bid each other good night and turn in for the last night, as we supposed, in Geyser Land.

HOT SPRING CONE, IN YELLOWSTONE LAKE.

I had noticed that during the evening Mrs. Cowan was uneasy, and upon being asked what was wrong, replied "nothing." Yet I was not satisfied, and as I lay there, I could see her occasionally come to the door of the tent and look out into the woods. I lay awake for a time, but about twelve o'clock dropped asleep.

We were beneath the trees, Arnold and Myers being together beneath one tree about eighteen feet from the camp fire, Mann and Dingee about eight feet nearer the fire rolled in their blankets, and Oldham and myself next to them. Cowan, Mrs. Cowan and Ida were in the tent, fifteen or twenty feet to the right, nearer the woods. How well I remember every incident of that evening. Little did we think that, as we slept, three red devils were within fifty feet of us, and had been watching our antics from the shadows of the trees.

DEPARTURE OF THE PARTY.

At daylight Dingee and Arnold are up and build camp fire preparatory to getting breakfast. As it grows lighter, Dingee takes the coffee pot and pail to bring water from a little stream in the edge of the timber, near Thud Geyser. He has not gone but a few yards when, looking towards the southwest, he saw within fifty yards of him, three Indians sitting upon their horses quite still. Seeing that they were discovered, they moved towards camp, each saying "How, how?" Dingee answers "How?"

They come into camp and Arnold came and woke Oldham and myself, saying:

"Frank, get up quick, there are Indians in camp!"

I jump to my feet and ask:

"How many?"

"Three," he replies.

"What are they?"

"I don't know, but think they are Nez Perces."

"Wake the balance of the camp, except Emma and Ida," I said, but the precaution is not needed, as I can see Mrs. Cowan looking through the folds of the tent at the Indians.

As I am dressing I hear Dingee ask the Indians:

"What are you?"

"Snake Injun," one replied.

"No Snake Indian," says Dingee, to which they made no reply.

The camp is nearly all up and I go towards the Indians and say "How?" They each respond "How?"

I address the one nearest me and ask:

"What tribe?"

"Me Nez Perce," he replies.

"What band?" I again ask.

"Looking Glass' Band," he answers.

Leaving the party to question them I go to the tent and find Mrs. Cowan crying quietly.

"Is there any danger, Frank?" she asks.

"I do not know, but hope not. Is George awake?"

"No."

I tell her to awake him and open the tent. Cowan is now awake and I tell him we are going to have some trouble. Ida is aroused by our conversation, and cautioning both her and Emma not to show themselves, I go back to where the boys are interrogating the Indians. Arnold tells me that the Indians want flour, bacon, sugar, etc., and I sit down to talk with them. Addressing one of them, I ask:

"What is your name?"

"Me Charley," he replies.

"Where is the balance of the Indians?"

"Down there not far," (pointing southwest towards the east fork of the Fire Hole,) "camped on river down there."

"How many?"

"Three, four hundred."

"Who chiefs?"

"Looking Glass, Joseph, White Bird, chiefs. Joseph, he towards lake, three days," meaning that Joseph was towards Henry's Lake about three days march.

"Will they fight party?" meaning ourselves.

"Don't know, maybe Injuns come steal horses, maybe kill. Don't know."

"Will chief kill citizens?"

"No, chief no kill you. No kill you, friends."

Cowan now comes up and says "How?" and asks them some questions about who they are, etc. They keep their eyes on the tent while talking, and leaving the boys to keep them engaged, I motion to Cowan, and we walk to one side to decide what course to pursue. We are convinced from what has been said, that they mean us harm, and we conclude to keep Emma and Ida concealed, and send the Indians off as soon as possible. Cowan goes into the tent and I return to camp, when Charley says:

"Injuns no kill, no fight, chiefs no kill you; no kill you, friends."

"We stay here?" I ask.

"Don't know, maybe some Joseph's Injuns come up here, kill you, maybe want horses. Heap mad, Joseph's Injuns."

"How many bad Indians?"

He replied by holding up both hands three times, meaning thirty, ten each time. He says:

"Joseph's Injuns heap bad."

Arnold and Dingee have gone on the hill back of camp to see if they can get a sight of the other Indians that Charley says are encamped near us. The Indians again make a demand for coffee, bacon, etc., but Cowan does not propose to give it to them. Upon this, one of the other Indians gets up and moves back a little ways and places his hands to his mouth and tries to whistle through his thumbs. Cowan grabs his needle gun and says:

"Here, none of that. Keep your hands down!" at the same time motioning him to keep his hands by his side. Charley turns around and speaks to the Indian in their native tongue, and he comes back and sits down.

I ask Charley if they saw an old man down the creek. He replied:

"Yes. Injuns got him prisoner now. Catch him last night."

"How did you know our party was here?" I asked him. Pointing to the other Indians and himself he answers:

"We go out watch. See big fire, come up. See you all time. Watch you all night in woods. Injuns watch 'em heap all night. You heap big time," pointing to our party and referring to our jollification of the night before.

Arnold and Dingee now return and report Indians in every direction below us, looking at the geysers. We all hold a consultation and decide that we had better not move. Some think we had better stand them off, but all agree to getting the horses, and three or four go out for that purpose while the remainder watch the Indians.

I proposed to Cowan that he and I ride down to see the chiefs and ask that we be allowed to return home without molestation. Cowan does not approve of the plan, but upon my representing that had they intended to kill us, they could have easily done so during the night without fear of retaliation, he admits that it may be advisable to go, and finally gives his consent. I ask Charley what he thinks of my going to see the chiefs, and if he thinks we will be allowed to return. He answers:

"Don't know. *Maybe* so. Maybe Injun kill. Don't know."

There is evidently no satisfaction to be had from this fellow, and we make ready our horses to go down and determine the question by experience.

As we are about to set out, Mrs. Cowan comes to us and begs us not to go, and says that if we go, all should go together. The Indians have arisen and are talking together, and pointing to the ladies. There is deviltry in their eyes, and as Cowan looks toward them he picks up his needle gun. I tell him not to shoot yet, to wait awhile. The boys are all in with the horses now, and the Indians keep asking for flour, bacon, etc. Two of them have stepped over to Harmon's camp to beg, Dingee and Arnold have gone up on the hill, and Mann coolly gets the coffee pot and proceeds to get breakfast. I remark that I doubt if there is a healthy appetite in the party, that of the Indians excepted, and Mrs. Cowan remonstrates with him for cooking at such a time as this. Mann replies that it is getting late, and we might just as well eat as not, but adds, " if you don't want any breakfast let us pack up and move out of here." That's my sentiments exactly, and Mann and Myers give the Indians some bacon and flour to keep them quiet. Oldham and myself proceed to harness the horses, and we conclude that we will pull out down through the main encampment and take our chances. We all assist in getting ready to move, and as Dingee and Arnold are still out, I halloo for them to come in. They do so, and report Indians all around us, but think that they have not discovered us as yet. Arnold is opposed to our going, but as we are all ready, he reluctantly consents and gets into the buggy with Mrs. Cowan and Ida. Mann and Myers take the wagon; Oldham, Dingee, Cowan, Harmon and myself mount our horses, and, taking the three Indians with us, we break camp, and file out about nine o'clock.

7

Dingee's prophecy is about to be fulfilled; he is already visibly affected with emaciation.

The three Indians are marched ahead, with Oldham on one side, Dingee on the other, and Cowan immediately behind them. The carriage follows next, with Harmon and myself following it, and the wagon brings up the rear. We, you may be sure, each grasped our guns. I have a good needle gun with eight rounds of ammunition, Harmon has a Henry rifle with two hundred cartridges, Cowan has a good needle gun with thirty rounds of ammunition, Myers has my shot gun, Mann has a Ballard rifle and a revolver, Dingee has a good revolver, and Oldham has a Ballard rifle, but with only three rounds of ammunition, and a small revolver. These, with our hunting knives, which all carry, constitutes the sum total of our weapons of defence.

The Indians have one needle gun, two Henry rifles, and are well supplied with ammunition and knives.

As we leave the grove of pines, where we were encamped, we have, for a mile and a half, a piece of swampy marsh land, in front, to the left, and off to the right, extending in all two and one-half or three miles from north to south. We had not left the timber more than two hundred yards when we ascended a little rise in the marsh, from which we see the Indians on the move up the east fork. As far as we could see, up and down the river, they were moving abreast in an unbroken line ten or fifteen feet deep, driving ponies and constantly riding out and in the line. We could see about three miles of Indians, with one thousand or fifteen hundred ponies, and looking off to the left we could see more Indians looking at the geyers in Fire Hole Basin.

As we came out into full view upon the rise, there was a commotion along the line, and we could see the warriors drop out and gather into groups of, perhaps, thirty or forty each, and stood looking towards us. We contined our course south-west, in almost an opposite direction from that of the Indians, which was north-east. They watch us for a time, when of a sudden, with one impulse seemingly, they come pell-mell, whooping and yelling like a band of fiends. Emma and Ida beg of us to shoot them rather than let them fall into the hands of such demons. Cowan rides up to Charley and tells him to stop the Indians from coming closer. Charley acts upon the hint and rides out and warns them back, and we stop our wagons. As our little band gather together in the face of such overwhelming numbers, there is a strange glitter in their eyes, and it is evident that they will not go down without sending several yelling red devils to the " happy hunting grounds " as a partial recompense.

The Indians check up, and finally halt about one-fourth of a mile from us. They number about seventy-five or eighty warriors. I propose that we keep on our way, and we again start. We encounter Indians coming and going in every direction, and as fast as we come up to them they follow along with us, and before we know it they have us completely surrounded. We have now reached the east fork, and on crossing it we have but a mile to go before we strike the timber land on our route home. The Indians cross with us, and allow us to proceed about a half-mile further, when they order us to stop. We dismount, and ask them what they want. But they make no reply, and keep riding around us, varying the proceeding occasionally by galloping to and fro in front of us. As our party glance frequently at Mrs. Cowan and Ida, who are crying quietly, I can see their eyes snap and their hands play nervously with their guns. The Indians watch us constantly like cats, and keep their guns cocked and lying across their horses in front of them.

I turned to Charley, who has done all the talking so far, (the red devil keeps his eyes on Mrs. Cowan all the time) and ask him why we were stopped, and why they keep us waiting there. He says that Looking Glass is coming pretty soon.

We wait here probably five minutes, when an old Indian comes up who tells us, through Charley, that Looking Glass wants us to come back to him, and that Chief Joseph is coming with his Indians but a little ways off.

Charley tells our party to turn back, and that Looking Glass and White Bird will save us from Joseph's " bad Injuns." At this about thirty or forty of the Indians near us break off towards the timber in front of us, yelling and shouting as they go, and soon disappear in the timber.

Charley tells us to turn back quick, as the Indians have gone to tell Joseph's band to hurry up. We remount our horses, but I can see that our party don't care particularly to return, but we start back, inasmuch as we can't help ourselves. I thought that we would be safe could we but reach the chiefs, and hastened to turn the buggy and wagon, and retrace our course. We had got fairly started back, when we hear a noise in the rear, and directly here comes the Indians who had gone after Joseph, with their infernal " yip, yip, yipping."

They ride up behind us and urge us forward by saying, "Quick, fast. Heap fast," and as they ride around us on all sides they throw the ends of their lariat at the horses in the wagon and buggy and we start on the run with the Indians all around us, laughing and shouting, and telling us that Joseph is coming. We go in this way for a time then turn off to the left and follow the main trail upon which we saw the Indians moving when we first left camp. The devils keep "whooping us up, plenty," having lots of fun among themselves, seemingly at our expense. We strike the east fork now and are on a full run again. Mrs. Cowan and Ida are considerably frightened and Dingee is evidently losing his appetite.

We continue in this manner for three or four miles, when we come to fallen timber lying across the trail and we see that we are compelled to abandon our wagons, as we cannot travel farther with them. The party halts and we proceed to unhitch the horses and saddle them for Mrs. Cowan and Ida to ride. The Indians are all around us watching every movement and constantly telling us to hurry.

While the boys are busy saddling up, I propose that I ride ahead and see if I cannot see Looking Glass and White Bird, and get the party out of this scrape. Oldham wishes to go with me, but I tell him I will go alone, and request him to stay with the party. I turned to an Indian near me, who had a large red bandana handkerchief tied about his forehead with the knot in the rear, and ask:

"Will you take me to Looking Glass?"

"Yes, yes," he replies, "you give me cartridge."

"All right," I answer.

"How many you give?"

"How many do you want?"

"Five or six."

"All right," I reply, and bidding our party good bye, and telling them to hurry up to the chiefs as soon as possible, we start ahead.

We have overtaken the main body of Indians and we travel as fast as the trail and Indians will permit. We cross the river and try to get by the Indians but without making much headway. We travel in this way for a mile or so when my guide proposes that we cross the river and take a cut-off saying that he guesses that Looking Glass has gone up to the head of the column. He turns his horse across the river and I follow. The mare I am riding is uneasy and it is with difficulty that I urge her into the stream. We cross and take to the timber, and are now about a half mile from the other Indians who are on the opposite side of the river.

As we are riding along, my guide tells me that he is a brother of Looking Glass, as Looking Glass married his sister. He says that the citizens killed his squaw and papoose at the Big Hole fight, and concludes a history of his troubles by saying he is "heap mad."

I tell him that when he catches the fellows that killed his squaw to "whoop 'em up plenty," but that my friends and I were not to blame.

"Me heap mad. Me no like white man," he replied, and candor compels me to admit that there was no loss of love between us.

Directly he stopped short, and said his horse could go no farther, and said:

"You give me cartridge, and go on. You find Looking Glass up there little way."

"All right, but you must show me Looking Glass."

"No," he said, "my horse tired. Me no go."

We argued the matter for a time, and finally compromised by my agreeing to go ahead, and then his horse would follow.

He turned out of the path to let me go by, and I started to pass him and take the lead, thinking of no danger from him, at least. Just as I was about to pass him I saw him drop his hand on his revolver. I took the hint, stopped my horse, and as I was yet in the rear I quickly brought my needle gun into good position for that red bandana and said:

"Look here, my friend, you go now. You take me to Looking Glass and hurry up, too!"

He looked around, but seeing that

I HAD "THE DROP" ON HIM,

hurriedly said:

"Me go, me go!"

"You go fast, too. No stop. You stop me catch you, you bet!"

"No stop, you bet," and we "lit out" on a lope, his horse showing no disposition to tire. He did'nt stop again. As we rode along I thought I had never, with all my weakness, made such a fool of myself as I did this time. I was mad. To let that blood thirsty devil coax me out there alone for a target. His scheme was well planned, and it was only by the merest chance that he was foiled in his designs. It gave me a lesson in one phase of the Indian character,. and I learned it quickly and well. It is this: Never trust a red skin.

We proceeded now at a canter until we came to where Arnold, Dingee and myself had encamped for dinner the day before. Here is an opening where the Indians are going into camp for dinner. Looking Glass was not here yet, but we dismounted to wait for him. My guide grew very anxious about his cartridges, but I thought it would be a good idea to keep them from him until I saw Looking Glass. So I told him he could have them when he showed me the chief, but not before. The Indians began to gather around us now and as they were getting too familiar to be entertaining, I backed out of the crowd and stood upon the outside of the ring.

As I was standing near watching the maneuvers of the crowd, I was approached by an Indian whom my guide introduced as Looking Glass. I offered my hand and said "How?" He accepted it and returned the salutation "How, how?"

LOOKING GLASS

is a man of medium height, and is apparently forty-five years of age, his hair being streaked with grey. He has a wide, flat face, almost square, with a small mouth running from ear to ear. His ears were decorated with rings of purest brass, and down the side of his face hung a braid of hair, adorned at the end with brass wire wound around it. The ornament worn by him, that was most conspicuous, was a tin looking-glass, which he wore about his neck and suspended in front. From this he gets his high sounding and reflective title. He wore nothing on his head and had two or three feathers plaited in his back hair. This was his appearance to me, although my inventory of his stock of attractions was a hasty one. I asked:

"You friend?"

"Yes, citizens friend."

He then asked me who I was, and as I was about to explain to him why our party were in the basin, and the object of our coming, I was interrupted by the appearance of a half-breed and old man Shrively. Shrively introduced the half-breed as

WHITE BIRD,

and asked me questions concerning the party.

White Bird, (or more properly Joe Hale, as that is his name among the whites, and the name by which I shall hereafter call him) now told me to come with him, and as Looking Glass had moved off, I started to follow, but was interrupted by my guide who again demanded his cartridges. I gave him six and he wanted more, but as I had but eight, I refused to give him more. Joe, seeing me give him cartridges asked me what I was doing, and I told him. He said:

"No give Injun cartridge, no give."

"Shall I take cartridges back?" I ask.

He smiled significantly as he said:

"My friend, *you no take 'em back*," and told me to come to his lodge. Shrively and I started to follow and as we walked after him Shrively gave me the particulars of his capture the night before, and how he had purchased his life by consenting to act as guide for them. I asked him what he thought of our situation, and he said he believed in fatality, and that if our time had come we would die. I did not jump for joy at this announcement, as I thought our time had certainly come, judging from what I had seen during the morning, and that we would most assuredly go hence soon.

Arriving at

JOE'S CAMP

I was told to unsaddle the mare, and having done so, Joe came up and relieved me from further duty in that line. I was told to sit down, and having nothing better to do, did so. Shrively having taken care of his horse, came and sat down by me on some robes and blankets. As Joe was off attending to some camp affairs, we had a conversation about our situation, and we agreed in thinking that matters were anything but promising. He asked after my sisters, and gave me all the encouragement he could as regards them, as he saw that their welfare was uppermost in my thoughts.

The Indians kept coming into camp, all driving their horses. As they came into camp the warriors would lounge around in the grass while the squaws would do the unpacking and unsaddling and make the preparations for dinner.

Presently Joe came back and said:

"Give me gun."

I handed it to him.

"What you do up here?"

I made him understand, by imitating the steam coming from the ground, that we had been visiting the geysers. I said:

"Can party go home?"

"Don't know," he replied, " me see Looking Glass and Joseph pretty soon. They see."

"Is Joseph here?"

"Yes; Joseph's Injuns, bad Injuns. They kill all time. Bad Injuns Maybe trade horses. Take'm you horses. You horses fat; my horses poor. Me swap. Give'm you good horses; my horses poor, but take'm you home."

I asked him if we should give up our horses would they let us go home.

"Maybe, my friend. We want you guns, you revolvers, all cartridges. Injuns maybe want blankets, saddles. Don't know. See bye'm-bye."

He asked me how long before our party would come up, and I told him they would be along "bye'm-bye. Indians got them way back. Be along bye'm-bye."

He told me to bring them into his camp when they came. He sat there looking at me for some time, and finally observing a ring on my finger said:

"Let me see'm you ring?"

I held out my hand to let him examine it. He said:

"No. Get'm off. Me want'm ring."

"No get'm off," I said.

"My friend, me see'm ring. Get'm off."

I told him I couldn't get it off; it fit too tightly; and I made an ineffectual attempt to remove it from my finger. He says:

"My friend, me get'm off," and he smiled seductively and convincingly as he took out his sheath knife and drew it across his finger.

I was not slow to take the hint, nor in benefitting by it. I put the ring in my mouth, and was astonished with the rapidity with which it came off, although it did take a part of the finger with it. I took it from my mouth, and politely handed it to him.

As the thieving devil slipped it on his finger, he incidentally remarked, "Heap good."

I, wishing to convince him of my magnanimity, said:

"Joe, I give you that ring. I present it to you as a slight token of my esteem. Please accept it."

He looked up and smiled complacently, but I could not tell from his manner whether he fully appreciated my generosity, but infer, from the significant wink of his left eye, that he did.

We had now been in camp a half hour, when I saw our party coming, surrounded by the Indians. I told Joe my friends were coming, and he said for me to bring them to his camp. I motioned for Cowan to come to us, and as they rode up I formally presented them to White Bird, who directed them to dismount and remove the saddles. They complied, and Joe and his Indians took the horses to the trees near by and tied them. While Joe was kindly taking charge of the horses, I conversed with the party, and they all thought, as I did, that our chances were dubious. Joe having returned, I told the party, in his presence and that of Shrively, whom all had greeted cordially, that Joe thought we could go if we would give up our guns, ammunition, etc. I turned to Joe and asked him if that was right, and he says:

"Yes, my friends. You all stay here. Me go see Joseph and Looking Glass," and he started around the encampment, which was in the form of a circle, and numbered four or five hundred Indians in all. He was riding Cowan's horse, and as he made the circuit of the camp he kept haranguing the warriors. I afterwards learned that he was hallooing, "watch out, look out," which was a caution to them not to let the soldiers surprise them.

Having made the round he rode to the other side of the encampment from us, where I presume Looking Glass and Joseph were encamped, as I saw a great many warriors ride up to where Joe entered the woods.

In about fifteen minutes Joe returned and told us that he would give us horses to go home with, but wanted us to "swap." He also said he wanted our guns, ammunition, etc., and as he offered

nothing in exchange for these, we supposed he *accepted* them as
" boot."

A HORSE TRADE EXTRAORDINARY.

Our party consulted upon the proposition made us, and as we couldn't do anything else, consented to take the crow with no requests for turkey.

The Indians, headed by Joe, now began the " swapping," and as it seemed to be altogether a one-side trade, it was soon finished. Their method was to take a horse, without even saying "swap" or no " swap," lead it away, and bring us back whatever they pleased. To Oldham, from whom they had taken two good horses, they brought a horse, very poor, and a little old mule, that had been shot through the shoulders. Oldham took the lariat of his mule, and, giving it a jerk, turned it around, and finally succeeded in getting it near Mrs. Cowan, to whom he remarked, " that this was the *easiest crowd to trade with* he ever saw." He stood and critically examined that mule from " stem to stern," as Skipper Dingee would put it, then, as a wave of unfathomable disgust swept over his features, he spoke through his foot in a way that was at once expressive and moving; at least it moved the mule about a rod. He stood looking at the mule's ears alternately flopping as it hobbled away, seemingly lost in deep reverie. Dingee aroused him by asking "Al, what do you think your little " Bunch of Roses" would say could she see you now?" It was too much, (mule,) and he walked away.

Cowan with Mrs. Cowan, Ida, and Shrively, were sitting by themselves during the "trading." Cowan sits smoking, never saying a word, except it be to encourage Mrs. Cowan, but watching carefully every motion of the Indians. Shrively is doing all he can to cheer Ida, and the rest of the party are walking back and forth impatiently waiting for the Indians to finish dividing the spoils.

Joe finally came to us and informed us that they had finished, and pointed out the horses we were to take. He told us to put our saddles on them, which surprised us, as we never expected such a courtesy. We hastily complied and were soon ready for the road, Emma retaining her side saddle and Ida riding in a man's saddle.

As we were about to depart I went to Joe and asked him for some bread for the white girls, and he stepped back to where his squaw was and obtained some for them. I gave it to the girls, but Mrs. Cowan did not eat.

They now robbed us of our guns except the Ballard rifle of Oldham's which he refused to give them. Charley, our interpreter of the morning, taking Dingee's six shooter, a splendid weapon, (and one that subsequently played a prominent part in the shooting,) which he appropriated to his own needs with considerable relish. Another Indian came to Dingee and asked him to swap blankets, holding up his dirty, greasy, single blanket, that he proposed exchanging for Dingee's extra double one. Dingee, with an eye to business says:

"No swap."

"Better swap. Take'm blanket any way," says the Indian, and Dingee with another eye to discretion, says:

"All right. Me swap."

Nobody has ever asked Dingee what induced him to make that trade, but he must certainly have had good reasons for making it. Dingee is shrewd. He may lose his appetite, but never his wits.

The Indians had finished their dinner and been on the move some time since, and the warriors now gathered round us and took our knives. They were moving over the mountains separating the Basin from the Yellowstone, by the same trail we had followed from the falls. Joe came to us and said:

"Get'm horses quick. Injuns come now. Bad Injuns come They getting mad now. You go quick, my friends. You go out in timber. Keep in timber, my friends. No go out of woods."

"Will we get away, Joe?" I asked.

"Yes, my friend. Me hope you get away, but Injuns heap mad."

I proposed that our party stay with him. He said:

"No, you go home now," and he came and shook us by the hand, saying:

"Good bye. Go quick."

As he passed Arnold and Dingee he told them to get away the best they could as "Injuns heap mad. They kill maybe."

He came to Mrs. Cowan and Ida, and shaking their hands said:

"Good bye, my friends, good bye, my sisters."

He mounted his horse, (the one I had ridden, belonging to Mrs. Cowan,) and leaning over whispered to me:

"My friend, go quick. Me tell you now go quick; bad Injuns over there," pointing to the flats out beyond his camp. As he said go quick, he gave his horse a dig in the side, and away he went towards the head of the column on the trail going over the mountain, taking Shrively with him.

DANGER THICKENS.

Our party now started for the timber and when we had gone about thirty or forty yards, we looked back and saw the Indians following us in two's and three's coming out on each side of us with their guns cocked ready for use. One glance was sufficient to show our party that we were in for a muss, but as I glanced at the party I could see no evidence of fear, only anxiety for Emma and Ida. I sincerely believe that throughout all our trials, this was the one thought uppermost in the minds of all.

Charley, with several other Indians, now came pretty close and told us to come out of the timber, and go home by the trail. It was swampy and mirey, with many warm springs and much fallen timber there. Our horses kept falling and stumbling, and I said to the party:

"Let us get out of this. If we have to be shot, let us get out where they can have a fair show to get us."

The boys were tired of this, and we turned and left the timber and struck the flat. As we came out we saw forty or fifty Indians above us two or three hundred yards, and as they saw us coming out of the timber they made a break for us and soon had us surrounded.

Charley spoke and said:

"Where balance of party?"

"All here," I replied.

"No, two gone."

I looked around and found that Arnold and Dingee were gone. I sincerely thanked God that they were away. I knew then that our friends would know how we had died.

Charley then spoke to the Indians, and some of them started off into the woods. Turning to us he said:

"Two men get away. Injuns catch 'em now, kill 'em sure. No get away."

I think that there was a silent prayer from the hearts of every one, for their safety.

The Indians had now surrounded us and were jabbering away among themselves when I turned round and asked Charley what they proposed doing with us.

"*You go home pretty soon*," he answered. Saying something to the Indians they separated for us to go through down the trail towards the wagons.

THE FIRST SHOT.

We started down the trail, the Indians meanwhile sitting on their ponies watching us, and we had got but a few rods, when we heard shots in the woods near where we supposed Arnold and Dingee were.

"There go Dingee and Arnold, poor fellows," we exclaimed.

The compressed lip and flashing eye said plainer than words could express it, "Oh if we only had guns now!" It is fortunate that we did not have them or there would have been none left to tell this tale.

Hearing the guns, the Indians, with a yell, started for us again, and we stopped and waited for them to come up. Emma and Ida were crying quietly, but not a sound escaped their lips to tell of their terror. It was pitiful to look in their eyes and see the anguish of mind reflected in their depths. My heart bled for my poor helpless sisters.

The Indians rode to us and began jostling, laughing, shouting, and running against us. Soon another squad of the cowardly devils came up and joined in the hellish fun, and kept pointing their cocked guns at us.

Finally Charley said that Joseph wanted us to come back, and I proposed to the party that we go back to the chief, and we again turned and started back, the Indians following us laughing and jostling us as we went.

We had gone about two hundred yards when they again stopped and demanded our saddles and blankets, which we gave them, and one Indian dismounted and pulled a revolver out of Mann's boot. Mann, with more indignation than it is possible to express in words, shouted, "You take it. Take everything, you d——d hog!"

They then told us to get on our horses again and come along. As we did so a number of the Indians broke off and entered the timber, but there was still forty or fifty surrounding us. As we reached the edge of the timber we were told to get together in a group. A little chief, who wore a drummer's jacket and was riding a large black horse, now took command, and I noticed that the other Indians obeyed him implicitly. They kept riding around and around us telling us to get close together, and they would significantly feel each other's pulse and laughingly point at us. We understood them.

We did not obey them in getting together, knowing well what it meant. The little chief coming near me I begged him to let the party go, as we had nothing to fight with, I said:

"No fight, no fight. Nothing to fight with."

He looked at me a moment and said:

"Get 'em together," pointing to the party.

I looked around and saw that the party were all mixed in among the Indians. I to spoke them, saying:

"BOYS, DON'T GET TOGETHER."

I particularly noted the appearance of Cowan, who was quietly sitting upon his horse, but with an expression of deadly hate in his eye that I never can forget.

The hooting and yelling painted devils surrounding us, toying with us, ere they took the life-blood for which they thirsted. At such a time one is almost forced to believe that there is no justice in heaven.

We waited here some ten minutes for the killing to commence, knowing, by the expression of their faces, that it was inevitable. I finally turned to the party and said: " Let us try to get to Joe." We started, but the Indians shouted, " No go," and the little chief rode in front of me. I shouted again, " Yes, we go. You kill, kill now. No care," and I did not care, as I thought that killing was their game, and the sooner it was done the better.

We began to move, and as the chief had ridden in front of me I turned my horse to the left and rode up beside him, he having in the meantime turned his towards mine. We rode side by side some distance when he stopped both our horses and let our party pass. We fell in behind them, and had advanced but a few rods when we heard two shots about thirty or forty yards ahead of us, and I heard Mrs. Cowan scream:

"O, George! O, George!"

The little chief then made a break to the left upon the side of the mountain above the trail, taking my horse with him. He dismounted, tied his horse to a sapling, took his gun from his belt, and started on a run down to the place of shooting leaving me there. In about five minuter after, I heard shots in different directions, and saw Indians plenty as the trees, and running in every direction. I could see Mrs. Cowan a few feet in front of me kneeling by Cowan and crying, "O, George, O, George." Quite a crowd of Indians had collected about them, and presently I saw Ida running and screaming with the Indians after her. She kept screaming, and made a dash through the Indians and got to where Cowan and Mrs. Cowan were. I could hear Mrs. Cowan pleading for them "to kill her (Mrs. C.) too, to kill her first!"

Meanwhile the Indians kept running backwards and forwards, shouting all the time, and yelling as they thought they had shot one of our party. At the first fire, it seems that the party broke, every one doing for himself. No one of us could fight but Oldham, and he had been shot through the face at the first fire and was disabled. Cowan had been shot from the front, the ball passing through the thigh. The Indian that shot him had aimed at his body. Cowan, when shot, jumped from his horse and started for a ravine below the trail, but his limb being partially paralyzed, he fell over a fallen tree in his path, where Mrs. Cowan found him, she having jumped from her horse and broke through the crowd of Indians. The rest of the party had run towards the marsh, which, as before stated, was covered with willows and high grass. The Indians following and shooting at them.

In looking down towards where Cowan was, I saw a group of Indians in great commotion. Supposing that Cowan and all were killed I looked around to see some chance for escape. I found I was entirely surrounded by Indians who were watching me with guns in their hands, waiting for me to make a break when they would have shot me as I ran. I stooped down on the neck of my horse intending to leap to the ground when I saw guns raised all about me to shoot. I thought my time had come and straightened up on my horse expecting to feel a bullet crashing through me instantly. I really felt anxious for it to come, and relieve my suspense. All this occurred in less time than it takes to write it yet it seemed ages to me at the time.

As I raised up I happened to glance off to the left where I saw the young chief who had left his horse beside me, standing in a little thicket close at hand. He was in a stooping posture with his gun raised to his face about to fire. If there is a period in a man's life when he thinks rapidly, I believe it is at such a time. I thought that many of these Indians were Catholics and it suddenly occurred to me to make the sign of the cross. What impelled me to do so I know not. It was a sudden impulse that prompted me and it was as suddenly put into execution.

Instantly his gun was lowered and running to his horse he untied it, sprang upon it, and casting a hasty glance about us at the Indians, said to me.

"Come quick. Me no kill you."

I followed him and found that our course led past the crowd collected about Cowan. As we were about to pass I saw Mrs. Cowan wringing her hands and could hear her cry:

"O, my God! George, O, George!"

I could hear Ida crying "George, George, Emma, Emma!"

I jumped from my horse and broke through the crowd of Indians to where Mrs. Cowan and Ida were kneeling beside Cowan. I saw Cowan reclining upon his left elbow and he seemed to recognize me about the same time that I saw him. I was then probably about four feet from him and as I approached he said:

"Frank, for God's sake get me some water!"

I glanced around and saw that we were entirely hemmed in by Indians, and I said:

"George, I can't. We are all gone, there is no show for any of us."

He raised himself upon his hand and said:

"O, God, won't some one get me some water?"

Mrs. Cowan made a move as if to get up when I felt a touch upon my shoulder, turned and found it was the young chief who was standing close at my side. He spoke to me in a low tone, saying:

"Come quick, Injun kill now. Come quick."

I followed him and passed through the crowd of Indians who were still running around here and there like a swarm of bees. He led the way back to our horses which were standing as we left them, and mounting, motioned me to get on my horse, saying:

"Come quick. Bad Injuns kill now. Come quick."

He took the lead and I followed up the trail. We had gone perhaps fifty yards when he turned suddenly into the ravine or marshy place and beckoned me to follow. I ran my horse into the thicket after him, rode up beside him and began to tell him "not to kill white girls," when he held up his hand and motioned me to keep quiet. The Indians were still shooting all around us it seemed, and they would give a yell occasionally when they had hit one of our party, as I supposed.

We had been in the thicket probably three or four minutes, when, on looking through the bushes, I saw the Indians in a great commotion again surrounding Cowan and the girls. As I looked I heard another shot and a scream from Emma and Ida. I turned to my chief and begged him not to kill white girls, and crossed myself as I said it. He replied:

"No kill, no kill. Injun take'm white girls prisoner. No kill white girls. Take'm white girls, make'm squaw. No kill."

"Will Indian kill me?" I asked.

"Don't know, maybe. You no go, you stay me. You my prisoner. Me no kill you. Me no like white man. Kill'm my friends. Kill'm my squaw, my papoose, my friends in Big Hole fight. Me no like you."

Looking at me a moment he crossed himself and said:

"Me catlic, you catlic."

The reader may be assured that I did not fail to keep that impressed upon his mind thenceforth.

I heard no more from Mrs. Cowan or Ida, and I could see that the Indians were dispersing. We remained where we were for about ten minutes or until matters had quieted down. We could hear an occasional shot in the distance, but there seemed to be no Indians in our immediate vicinity.

The chief, after a time turned to me and said:

"Come, you drive'm horses. My horses."

All right," I said, and he having pointed out the horses I was to drive, I immediately adapted myself to my

NEW VOCATION

and made myself generally useful, rest assured.

The Indians now began to come back, the squaws driving the ponies first this way then that. They seemed to be wandering aimlessly about, when the chief turning around, asked me if I knew the trail, pointing towards the mountains, I replied yes, when he said:

"Injun lost. Don't know'm trail. You know'm trail?"

"Yes."

"Show'm trail."

I motioned for him to come with me, and we crossed the ravine and a little creek that comes down from Mary's Lake. Here the two trails come near together. I told him that both trails went over the mountain to the Yellowstone, and showed him by pointing, that the one leading north went by Mary's Lake but the one to the north-east did not. These trails run nearly parallel, at no place being over four miles apart. He asked:

"Which way Injuns go?"

"Go either way. Some go one way, some go other way," and explained that the trails met on the other side of the mountain about twelve or fifteen miles.

He looked steadily at me for a moment then said:

"Show'm trail," motioning for me to take the right hand road.

There were quite a number of Indians gathered about us by this time, waiting to be shown the trail, and I took the lead and soon had them all following on the trail to the north-east. The chief then stopped me and said:

"Wait, you drive'm horses."

"All right," I said, and we stopped by the side of the trail waiting for some of the squaws to bring up the horses. Every now and then as the squaws, with the ponies and young Indians, were passing us, a little devil, fifteen or sixteen years old, would stop opposite us, raise his gun, cock it, and, pointing it towards me, would say:

"G—d d—m; G—d d—m! No good. White man no good;" then they would look at each other and laugh uproarously. I will admit that I couldn't see where the laugh came in. It made me nervous. So nervous, in fact, that I resolved, then and there, if I ever got out of this scrape and should catch one of those imps, I would sit down on him, dig out his ears with a knife, and pour in the Lord's Prayer. Even after passing me, they would come back, where I was busily driving horses, and go through the same antics. I tell you those devilish little Indians made me more nervous than I ever was before or have been since. I could not see that future generations were to be benefitted or civilization, in any degree, advanced by such practices, hence prefer, that in having such fun, they select another subject in the future.

The horses having come up the chief told me to help him drive them and not to " go way. Injuns kill. Stay me." Telling him, " No go. Me stay, *you bet*," we started up the mountain.

About a mile from where the shooting had taken place, I looked back and saw a white woman riding on a horse behind a big Indian. I did not recognize her, and supposed it was another captive they had made before capturing us. I kept on driving the horses, backwards and forwards across the trail, yet kept my eyes on the woman coming behind us. I did not think it was Mrs. Cowan, as when I last saw her she wore a blue waterproof cloak, while this woman was dressed in light colored clothing. A turn in the trail, however, brought us closer together, when I saw that it was Emma. I said:

" Emma ! "

She looked up and cried:

" Oh, Frank ! thank God you are alive."

She looked at me with such a look of horror depicted in her sunken eyes, as I hope I may never see upon the face of any human again.

" Where is Ida ? " I asked.

" I saw her taken off by the Indians, and think she is with them somewhere."

" Are any of our party alive ?"

" No; they are all killed. None got away I think. Oh, it is horrible. They killed George. They shot him through the head, and I had my arms around his neck. Frank, it is killing me. I can't stand this much longer."

" Did you see Al. ?" (Mr. Oldham.)

I saw him shot and fall off his horse. He jumped, threw up his hands and fell. The Indians followed him down into the ravine, and I heard them shoot once more. Oh, Frank, it was horrible, horrible. I wish I were dead."

"Emma, was there no show for any of the party getting away down there?"

"No," she said, "they were all killed." Pausing a moment, she continued:

"As this Indian lifted me on to the horse, I saw an Indian standing over George with a big rock in his hands. I saw George raise his hand to his head and the Indian then threw the stone on him, striking him on the head and crushing the skull all in. Oh, Frank, it was horrible. I have begged the Indians to kill me but they won't do it. What shall I do? I don't recollect anything more after the Indian threw the stone, until you spoke."

I kept telling her to keep up. We would get together again.

"What are they going to do with us, Frank?" she asked.

"I don't know. Since we have lived this long, I have hopes that we may get out all right," I replied. She continued, saying: "Frank, if they kill you, what shall I do? What shall I do?"

We had been riding about fifteen or twenty feet apart, and our conversation was carried on as I rode in and out among the horses which I was busily driving.

CHARLEY'S WORK.

Emma was riding behind Charley, the Indian who had come into camp in the morning, and was his prisoner. I saw then, what I before suspected, that he was the author of all the mischief. During all our trials of the day I had noticed that he kept his eyes on Emma, and now, in the culmination of our misery, I could see the realization of his hopes. Did you ever thirst for the warm heart's blood of a human? If not you can not imagine how intensely I hated that devil then. How I longed for my gun, and with what supreme satisfaction I could have scattered his brains to the winds. I thought that I saw a beloved sister subjected to a fate a thousand times worse than death. I doubt if God himself, the embodiment of love, would chastise me for harboring such thoughts as I did then.

Charley now stopped his horse and we were separated and I could not see her any where. We had by this time gone some two or three miles up the mountain when the chief motioned me to drive the horses out into an opening. I did so and he began counting them. Suddenly, he broke away on a run through the woods, without so much as saying "good bye," or with your permission." I was displeased with his uncivility, and (with a vivid recollection of those little red devils who kept pointing their guns at me) I struck out full tilt after him. Away we went, pell mell, through the thickets, brush and boughs, scratching my face, tearing my clothes, and knocking me around generally. I kept close to him, and just as I began to doubt his sanity, and to wonder "what in the thunder is up, and where is he going to?" we rode out into an opening where there were a number of loose horses, and he stopped. He had not heard me following him, and happening to look around and see me, he laid his head back on his shoulders and gave one of the most self-gratifying laughs I ever heard. It was a little louder and longer than the solemnity of the occasion required I thought, and I began to think that we had struck the jolliest band that ever cut a throat. He ceased laughing after a time, and looking at me with one of his most significant winks that blended coquetishly with the archness of his smile said:

"You heap stay, *heap* stay!"

"Yes heap stay; heap stay me. You *bet; plenty!*"

"All right. Drive'm horses. My horses!" pointing to the horses in front of us.

Again I fell to work, making myself more than useful. We were still among the Indians and it seemed to me that the whole country was alive with them and ponies. I drove some ponies up the trail a little ways and then came back to the horses which he had counted by this time.

We had gone some distance when a large Indian rode up behind us, whom I guessed was another chief, and to whom my "boss" began to laughingly relate the particulars of our trip hrough the woods, concluding with the remark, "him heap stay." The large chief kept his eyes on me, and during the time I think I never threw my whole soul into a work more completely, than I did this. I know I was much busier than any body else. They must have thought I liked it.

I could see the two talking together as they rode side by side and saw my " boss" make the sign of the cross and point towards me. This apparently satisfied the big chief, as he rode up to me and said:

" How ?"

" How ?" I replied.

" How far Yellowstone?" he asked:

" Fifteen miles; maybe more. Fifteen or sixteen miles."

" You take pack horse. Lead'm."

AN INTRODUCTION.

Pointing towards a squaw who was leading both a pack mule and a horse, he continued:

" My squaw. You lead'm pack mule." Saying "all right," I rode up to the squaw and she handed me the mule's rope. I started ahead but the mule seemed to think I did not travel fast enough, and made a break to get by me but I crowded him off the trail. Again he started to pass me and made a dash between two trees and stuck fast. He struggled and twisted but could get neither backwards nor forwards, the pack holding him tight. This produced a good deal of merriment among the squaws, and pointing at me, they kept saying, "Heap squaw, heap squaw. No good."

This riled me, and getting off my horse, I brought that mule such a welt across the nose with the end of the rope that he sat right down backwards and turned clear over, leaving the packs between the trees.

The two chiefs rode up and with the help of the squaw placed the pack upon the mule again. They insinuated that I had not better try that again, gave me the halter and we started ahead.

A mile farther brought us to the top of the divide, where Satan was burning brimstone and pumping steam with such infernal ingenuity. One of the chiefs rode back to where I was and pointing to a small fissure in the ground beneath our horses from which the steam was escaping, asked:

" What make'm steam?"

" Heap fire down under the ground," I replied, and motioned for him to pick up a piece of the hot sulphur lying loose about the fissure. He sprang from his horse and picked up a piece and began a critical examination of it. I told him to smell it. He p'aced it to his nostrils, gave a good snuff and dropped it with a look of disgust, (it was the first time I ever knew an Indian to be disgusted with a smell.)

"Ugh!" he said " No good, no good. What make'm?"

" Fire down below," I answered.

" Down there?" he asked, stamping the ground which gave forth a hollow sound.

" Heap fire down there," I said.

He jumped for his horse and with "No good, me go," struck out as hard as he could go. It was not merely a spirit of mischief that would have prompted me to have freely given five years of my life to have seen him drop through for a *few* minutes.

As we began the descent of the mountains the trail was much better and we moved ahead at a more rapid gait. It soon began to grow dark, and soon afterwards the sky became overcast with heavy clouds and it grew quite dark. The Indians kept asking how far it was to the Yellowstone, although we had yet some nine or ten miles to go. They seemingly had no idea of distance. We passed the place where we had camped on Monday and about two miles beyond and came to the creek where Arnold caught the little trout. Every thing that we had seen on our way to the Falls I noted now as we passed, and each incident, however small, was again recalled

Crossing this creek we soon came to another small creek where I asked the chief if I could get some water. He told me to get off and drink. I alighted and lay down to drink, still holding the halters of my horse and mule. The chief rode on and left me.

Here was my chance to escape. By crawling a few feet I could have lain down in the creek beneath the bank and waited for the Indians to have passed. There was no probability of their seeing me, as it was quite dark. All this passed through my mind while drinking, but as I thought of Emma and Ida, and the anguish they would suffer if I left them without their knowing what had become of me, I determined to remain. Rising, I mounted my horse and again started after my chief whom I soon overtook. As I rode up, he turned and said:

"Hello! no go much further."

He was evidently surprised to see me, and I concluded that he had purposely given me the chance to escape as he had done in the woods.

Ascending a little hill in the trail we could see ahead of us, what would have been, under any other circumstances, a beautiful scene. The Indians had encamped on the outer edge of a circular basin about three-fourths of a mile in circumference, and were building their camp fires about every twenty or thirty feet apart. The ponies, a thousand or more, were in the basin encircled by the fires. Others were constantly coming and we could hear their "yip, yip," as they drove the ponies in for unpacking. At any other time it would have certainly been picturesque.

I had lost sight of the chief who had saved my life and had been traveling with the other chief and his squaw until we came to the camp. As we entered I saw a group of squaws and Indians near us towards whom we rode and stopped. The chief said something to them and motioned me to dismount and unpack the mule, which I did immediately with the best of grace. Having removed the pack, the Indian took the horse and mule, and motioned me to sit down on the pack. As yet I had seen nothing of the girls coming into camp, although I kept watching the surrounding camp fires constantly, in hopes they would pass before them and thus reveal their whereabouts. Poor Ida! I had not seen her during the day, and I knew she must be suffering intensely, among the Indians somewhere near us.

INDIAN CAMP LIFE.

My chief now came back and touching me on the shoulder, said:

"Come, get'm wood."

I arose and followed him to the timber and began gathering sticks, etc., and having secured an armful, returned to camp. A squaw standing by, said to me:

"Mak'm fire."

She handed me a match and I soon had a good fire burning. The chief now told me to get some water, and as I did not know which way to go, he pointed across the encampment. I said "all right," and he gave me a coffee pot and a brass kettle in which to carry it. I started, but he shouted:

"Here, where you go?"

"Get water," I replied.

"You no go that way. Injuns kill," and he pointed to the Indians passing back and forth in the camp. Turning to another Indian lying near on the ground, he said something in the mother tongue. The Indian addressed, got up and came to us, when I saw that it was the chief that had saved my life. He came to me and partially removing his blanket, he placed the loose end around me, intending to go with me thus, after the manner of school girls. He held the blanket in this position with his left arm about my neck, but as I was opposed to such familiarity on so slight an acquaintance, I undid his affectionate clasp and got outside of the blanket. He said:

"No go that way, Injun kill sure," and removing the blanket from himself said:

"Here, you play Injun. Injun see'm you white man, kill you sure," and he wrapped the blanket around me.

"You Injun now," he said, "no kill now. Me go too," and taking the brass kettle from me, we started. He told me to keep the blanket over my head "like Injun," and we traveled ahead much after the manner of the illustrious ex-president of the ex-confederacy when he didn't escape. Notwithstanding the fact of my keeping the blanket closely pulled about my face, I nevertheless kept a sharp lookout for my sisters. As we were dipping up the water I asked the chief where the white girls were, and he said:

"Little white girl, she over there some where with Injun. Big white girl, she no come. Me no see'm. She come maybe, bye'm-bye."

We started for camp now, and as I could not get the Indian style of walking, the Indians that we passed looked at me pretty closely. My chief, though, kept his eyes open for mischief. We got back safe, and having deposited the water by the camp fire, I gave the blanket a toss on the ground. The odor was any thing but pleasant. The young chief seeing the action came and picked the blanket up, and handing it to me again, said:

"Put'm on blanket. Injun come pretty soon. Maybe kill you. Put'm on blanket and sit down there," pointing for me to be seated some distance from the fire, in order that the bright light might not reveal my presence.

Seeing Indians coming across the encampment, I followed his advice rather lively. From my position I had full view of the whole camp, and could see the squaws busily engaged in getting supper, while the noble red man lounged upon the grass. This kind of camp life was new to me, and had it not been for my anxiety for my sisters, I could have enjoyed it. To an observer under other circumstances, it would have been interesting, as it was, I took but little notice of what transpired around, being constantly on the alert to catch a glimpse of the girls.

As I sat there thinking of the events of the day, of the death of the boys whom I knew so well and regarded so highly, of the terrible fate of my sisters, and the inevitable death, as I supposed, in store for me, it all seemed more like a horrible dream than a reality. If there was any moment during all our trials that I gave way to human weakness, it was when I thought of our happiness of the night before when we were all together, full of bright anticipations of a pleasant journey home, and compared it with our present position. Then so full of life, now, six of the boys lying, mangled in the woods, cold in death. I thought, too, of the pleasant home circle. They, having heard of the Indian war, would certainly be solicitous as to our welfare. They would hear of our tragic fate, but what a horrible revelation would our bleaching bones make.

As I sat brooding over our fate, I heard the tread of an approaching pony, and on looking up I saw Emma being helped from its back. I sprang to my feet and as she came towards the fire I advanced to meet her. I extended my hand but she stepped back quickly. Throwing the blanket aside I said:

"EMMA, DON'T YOU KNOW ME?"

"O, God, Frank, is that you?"

I will not record the events of the next half hour. I only pray, reader, that you may ever be spared my experience during that time.

The Indians having supper now ready, one of them approached us and said:

"Supper, come."

Emma declined to go, and I motioned the Indian that we wanted nothing; he then told us to come near the camp fire and sit down there. We did so, and in talking of the events of the day, Emma asked if it was not possible to get Ida over where we were. I told her I did not think we could, but turning to one of the Indians near us I asked if "little white girl come over here?"

He said:

"No. Other Injuns got'm little white girl. Looking Glass Injun got'm."

"Whose prisoners are we?"

"Joseph's Injuns got'm you. White Bird's Injuns got'm her," pointing to Emma.

The Indians had now finished their supper and were squatting around the camp fire talking. One of the squaws again came up to Emma and asked her to eat.

Emma told her she wished nothing only some water. The

squaw brought it. Emma drank some of it, and bathed her face and hands in the rest, after which she felt better.

My chief came to me and pointing to an Indian sitting close by me, said:

"Him Joseph."

Joseph hearing him, turned partly around towards me. I said:

"Joseph!" and extended my hand.

He grasped it and gave it a shake. I asked:

"Friend?"

"Citizens friend," he replied.

I turned towards Emma, and said;

"My sister."

He extended his hand to Emma and said:

"You sister?"

"My sister stay with me?" I asked.

"Yes, you sister?"

"Yes."

"Yes, you sister. She stay here. You stay here. Stay in my lodge. Joseph's lodge. My house; Joseph's house. You sister, you, stay here all night."

As we were talking I noted carefully every feature of

CHIEF JOSEPH,

and suppose that he is a man about forty or forty-five years of age. He is about six feet high, broad shoulders, and of powerful *physique*. He is, also, intellectually well developed. He has a high forehead, a straight prominent nose, high cheek bones, and when he speaks he sets his lips together with a firmness that showed he meant what he said. He talked but little, but I noticed that when he spoke to an Indian, there was no hesitancy about obeying him. His son was pointed out to me, but I could see no traces of his father's qualities there. He was a careless, reckless, sort of a fellow, laughing and jabbering away with some of the young squaws. His father spoke to him once, when he arose quickly, without a word, jumped upon his horse, and was away in the darkness in a moment.

Shortly after my conversation with Joseph, one of the Indians came over to him and began talking. I could see by the gestures, of which their language is principally composed, that he was telling him of the troubles of the day. Joseph listened for a moment, then with a motion of disgust got up and went over where his squaw and grown up daughter were. He was evidently displeased with the actions of the Indians, in the shooting of our party.

The Indians now had nearly all arrived in camp, and we soon heard White Bird, or Joe, going his rounds again, and haranguing the Indians as he went, as at noon. He came near us, but not to the camp. He, it seemed, looked out for the camp regulations, such as appointing pickets, taking charge of prisoners, etc. I afterwards learned that Joseph and his band, and Looking Glass with his band, did the principal fighting.

Emma had now stopped crying, and we all sat around the fire. I could see the squaws frequently looking at Emma and pointing to her as they talked. A papoose was lying on a blanket near the fire, kicking away, in happy ignorance of what a mean little devil it was bound to make. I told Emma to take it up. Looking at me for a moment, she says:

"Me take that thing? I won't do it! I'd sooner die than take the nasty thing up!"

"That's all right on principle, Emma, but you take that papoose up. We are playing for our lives now."

Emma then motioned for a squaw to hand her the papoose, which she good-naturedly did, smiling and laughing as she placed it upon her lap. Emma immediately proceeded to wipe its nose, a no little job, rest assured. I saw this took with the squaws, and it certainly made an impresson upon them, so it did upon Emma, but with rather an opposite effect. As for myself, I know I could have sat down on that young one and smothered it, with a good deal of relish. Keeping the child but a few moments, Emma passed it back to one of the squaws, who again placed it on the blanket.

It was now getting late, and the Indians began to make down

their beds for the night. My chief and squaw made a nice bed for Emma and myself, of buffalo robes and furs, over which they spread a nice deer skin. They then motioned for us to come and lie down.

Telling Emma to cross herself, and how it had saved my life, we knelt together, and I know we both prayed fervently, if it was silently. The Indians were closely watching us the meanwhile. Having finished our prayers, we again crossed ourselves and lay down, and the Indians covered us with blankets and robes. They then made their beds around us in the form of a semicircle.

We covered our heads, and Emma again began crying and relating the particulars of the day's horrors.

She again gave me the particulars of the killing of her husband, and as she spoke of the Indian throwing the rock upon Cowan's head, it was all I could do to hold her. The shock had well-nigh crazed her. I did all I could to recall her mind from contemplating the horrors of the scene, but with no avail. She kept saying: " O, Frank, if they had not crushed his head with the stone. The blood spattered all around. O, Frank, it was horrible," and again she would spring up. I kept my arms clasped tightly about her, and it was a continual struggle with her all night long. The scene of the killing of Cowan was constantly before her, and as she thought of how he had died, begging for water, she would almost go into convulsions. I think no person could suffer more than she did then. My God! what a horrible night it was to me, too. How I longed for the welcome light of day.

Once during the night she became quiet for a time, and my chief, supposing we were asleep, came over to our bed, and kneeling down, slipped his hand beneath the robes and placed it upon my face. I grasped his hand, threw the cover from my face and asked him what he wanted.

" You sleep?"

" No sleep," I answered.

" You sister sleep?"

" No sleep," I said again.

"Me save you, you sister. Me send sister down river to-morrow."

Emma and myself had risen to a sitting posture when he had first spoken, and thanking him, and again crossing ourselves, we lay down.

Shortly it began to sprinkle when the chief and his squaw got up and getting a large wagon cover, spread it over us and tucked it in around us.

In about an hour after this, we heard one of the most mournful sounds that I ever heard. Emma started up and said:

"What is that?"

I listened for a moment, and told her:

"It is one of the Indians chanting for their dead."

We listened for a time, when it ceased. Those who have heard the death chant, know how mournful and weird it is, even under ordinary circumstances. But coming to us then it was inexpressibly doleful. It chilled to the marrow.

DAYLIGHT CAME AT LAST,

and at the first movement among the Indians we sat up. The Indians were soon astir, building camp fires and getting breakfast. As the day grows brighter we can see the Indians who were on picket coming in, and others going out to take their places. On looking to the south-east part of the camp we can see White Bird's camp, but can see nothing of Ida.

As we were looking in that direction, we saw an Indian ride suddenly out of the timber back of Joe's camp and come charging down through camp on a full run. He urges his horse to the utmost speed and passes us like a shot. As he passes, Emma exclaims:

"Look, Frank, he is riding Al.'s horse!"

She was right. It was Oldham's roan horse, Old Ranger, as Al. used to call him. The horse was a very fleet one, and I remarked to Emma if we only had two such horses as Old Ranger, we could leave our present company with little trouble. The sight of the horse again started Emma to crying.

9

The Indians came to us and wanted us to eat breakfast. Emma would eat nothing, but I finally prevailed upon her to take a little coffee. I sat down with them, and they gave me a spoon with a motion that told me to help myself. The meal consisted of nothing but a large dish pan full of cammas root cooked up like hominy, around which all gathered. It may be surmised that I hadn't a very hearty appetite, yet I concluded to make myself agreeable at any cost. I tasted the cammas root and think that it could be made palatable if properly cooked, but, as much as I dislike to comment upon the fare of my hostess, a love of truth compels me to admit that I have partaken of other meals with a greater relish. It looked like hominy, but the dirtiest hominy I ever saw, was clean compared with this. Grease, sticks, gravel stones, in short, dirt of all kinds almost, was here " lumped." I have *heard* of a sandy desert; here I *ate* a sandy dessert. It was food fit for an ostrich. Even Dingee could not have stomached it. I would commend it as a diet for Gen. Howard; he would then have more "sand in his gizzard." Not being hungry I took but a taste. The Indians then gave me a small piece of bread which I ate, and they then gave me some willow-bark tea in a tin cup, which I drank. The tea tasted well, but was rather sickening. I noticed they sweetened the water before adding the bark. The repast being finished, I crossed myself and rejoined Emma.

The sun was now up and as it threw its rays upon the tops of the surrounding mountains that were bright with the tinted leaves of early autumn, the scene was worthy an artist's brush. Everything seemed so calm and peaceful, I could scarcely realize the situation in which we were placed. Emma had changed so in appearance that one could not have recognized her as the cheerful, happy girl of twenty-four hours before. This was her first great sorrow, and it had made sad havoc of her youthful looks. The death of Cowan, under ordinary circumstances, would have crushed her, but to be a witness to his horrible fate was killing her. The day, too, the twenty-fourth of August, *was the second anniversary of her wedding day!*

Again Joe made the rounds of the camp, cautioning the Indians to be on their guard. As he came near our camp and saw Emma and myself, he rode up to us and said:

" Hello!"

" Hello, Joe."

He looked at us for a moment, then motioned for me to come to him. I did so when he asked:

" You prisoner?"

" Yes," I answered.

" You sister prisoner too?"

" Yes," I replied.

" How many you party gone?" he asked.

" Seven," I said.

" No, six," said he. " How many in party?"

" Ten."

" Nine in you party, six gone."

I explained that Harmon was not of our party but had joined us in the basin. He then asked me about the shooting of Cowan and Arnold. I told him all I knew, when he said:

" Too bad. Me tell Injun to let you party go home. G—d d——n Nez Perce. No good. They go back kill'm you friend. Me tell'm no kill. G—d d——n Nez Perce. No good!"

I then asked him about the little white girl. He said:

" Me no see'm her. She down there somewhere," pointing across the encampment. I asked if I could see her.

" Don't know," he said, " me see."

He then called Mrs. Cowan up, to whom he said "good morning." Mrs. Cowan returned the salutation, and he said something about the shooting of Cowan. He motioned us to go back, saying that he would come again " bye'm-bye." He conversed with the Indians a while, then started on his round again, haranguing them as before.

The Indians were now getting up their horses preparatory to moving on, and while thus engaged, Joe came back. Riding up to my chief he leaned over towards him and began talking in an undertone. As he talked I saw him point to me and I understood him to say:

KILL'M HIM TO-DAY. NO WANT'M HIM.

I sprang to my feet and went to where they were talking. I crossed myself and asked:

"Joe, you kill'm me?"

He said nothing, but looked at me with inhuman deviltry pictured in every lineament of his face.

I continued:

"Joe, you kill me to-day; me no care. But, Joe, let me tell you, no kill white girls. Me tell you, now, *no kill!* Got'm heap friends; *heap* friends. Live twelve years in Montana. Everybody know'm white girls. Joe, promise me you no kill'm white girls. Me tell you, now, *no kill'm.* Citizens come. Got'm heap friends, white girls."

For a half hour I begged and prayed for the life of my sisters. How earnestly I can not tell. You, kind reader, can only imagine.

During the time I could see nothing but stolid indifference, in his face. Not a look of sympathy, nothing but innate develishness could I see there. He finally turned to me and said:

"Me send you sisters home down Yellowstone river. Me give'm two white girls one pack horse, send'm down river, Yellowstone river."

"Alone?" I asked.

"Yes," he answers, *"they go alone!"*

"Joe, no send'm white girls alone. No find'm trail down river. White girls get lost. No go that way."

He then said he would "send Injun with them," which would have been a thousand times worse than alone.

"No, no! No send Injun," I said.

"Well, me see, me see," he replied.

I told him as regards myself, I did not care. He could do as he pleased. He said:

"Well, my friend, me see."

He now turned to go away, but I stopped him and again asked him what he was going to do with the girls.

He replied:

"Me don't know."

I then told him to take the girls to his camp and keep them there until they came to a white settlement or white persons, and to keep them with him always, and not let the other Indians get them. He promised to do so.

I said:

"Joe, you promise me?"

"Yes, my friend. You sister, my sister now. Me no kill'm you sister. Me take'm my camp, me keep'm. Bye'm-bye me give'm white friends. Me take'm my lodge. You sister, my sister."

Crossing myself, I told Joe to do the same, and said:

"Joe, you promise me," and crossed myself.

"Yes, me promise," and he crossed himself.

He told me to tell Emma to get up and come to him. She did so and he told her she was to come with him. Emma turned to me and asked me what they were going to do with us. I told her as briefly as I could the conversation we had had, and told her to stay in Joe's camp until liberated; never, under any circumstances whatever, to leave it, until she could do so with safety. I told her, also, if she and Ida undertook to escape and got away, to follow the trail down the Yellowstone, and they would come out all right.

I now bade her good-bye for, as I supposed, the last time. I had, then, no more expectation of ever seeing her again, than I have of dying before finishing this book. Of the next half-hour I will not write. Death, which I supposed inevitable, had no terrors for me, but the fate of my sisters, a thousand times worse than death, unmanned me. I had no idea that Joe would fulfill a promise. I would have willingly died to know that Emma and Ida were dead; yes, a thousand deaths, rather than that they should be subjected to such a fate—a squaw's life.

Joe now motioned for Emma to get upon the horse he was riding, Cowan's horse. He lifted her to a place behind him and rode off.

I presume I got reckless now, and it may be I was rather imprudent, if not saucy. I saw my chief was looking at me, and I went to him and said:

"I want to see the little white girl over there."

"No see'm," he replied.

"Yes; let me see'm little white girl. You kill me to-day. I no care. Let me see little white girl."

"No see'm. She go now pretty soon," meaning that she would go with the Indians which was about to move.

This made me mad, now, and I rather hotly said:

"Nez Perces Indians no good. Kill'm my friends; take'm white woman prisoner. No good. Me no fight. Got no gun. Nez Perces cowards. Shoot my friends like dogs. No good."

The chief continued smoking, and all the answer I got was a quiet smile, and,

"You go get'm you horse."

Handing me a rope, he said:

"He go with you," pointing to the young chief, who had befriended me the day before.

We started, and with the assistance of a couple of squaws, we soon had the horses of this outfit, some fifteen in number, in an opening by themselves. We, with some other Indians, surrounded them, standing about six feet apart. The "bucks" began lassoing such as they wanted to use during the day, and soon had caught all that they wished, except the horse of the chief—a large black horse, of unusual beauty and spirit—and the one he had ridden the day before. They soon caught the one I had ridden, and they told me to put a rope on him, which I did, and was about to lead him away, when one of the Indians told me to stop and help catch the chief's horse.

They made several unsuccessful attempts to lasso him, and he broke through the circle by me several times, as I was holding my horse and could not stop him. Each time he would pass, the

Indian next me would throw the lasso but miss him, and then we would have to all go and drive him back into the opening.

I asked the Indian next me to give me his lasso and I would "catch'm horse," which caused no little laughter. He gave me the lasso, however, and I took it, trusting to luck. I knew I could not do worse than what they had done, and sometimes luck succeeds where science fails. I knew how it should be thrown, and that, as Dingee asserted about sailing the boat, was assurance that I could do it.

The horse made a break to pass me, and, as he went by me, I threw the lasso over his head as neatly as it was ever done. Luck succeeded. As he reached the end of the rope I brought him up with a sudden jerk that certainly must have made him see stars. The Indians came around and said:

"Heap good. *Hi yu skook'um.* Heap good white man."

It was a "feather in my cap," that I tried to wear modestly, but I will admit to you, reader, confidentially, that I felt two inches taller than I did before. Fortunately there were no more horses to catch, as probably I could not have done the like again with a dozen trials.

The Indians were now stringing out over the hills to the Yellowstone, and as I looked I saw Ida and Emma. Ida had a white handkerchief tied over her head, but Emma still retained her hat. I saw Shrively, too, more than a mile away, in the file of Indians. I mentally bid them farewell, as I rode in among the Indians.

We had returned to camp with the horses, and they began packing up. I presume I was never busier in all my life than I was just then. The way I did throw those old traps together was astonishing. It may be inferred that I was nervous, too. I knew my fate had been decided, and I never expected to leave that camp, and when my chief came to me and said, "You get'm on horse," I got on that horse in a hurry, *you bet.* He motioned me to take the mule and lead it as I had done before, and I immediately fell in love with that mule and all the appertenances thereunto pertaining. I cannot say I like work, but I know I was never so anxious to do something useful in all my life. I would have willingly worked for nothing and boarded myself.

We were about the last to fall into line, and as we advanced we met warriors going back over the trail we had come the day before. I thought then if any of the boys had been so fortunate as to get away it was all up with them now.

I was riding along by the side of the chief's squaw, not having seen him since we started, when, on looking up, I saw him coming back. He came up and we stopped. The squaw said something to him, and he came on until within ten feet of me. The Indians near us had stopped, also, and were watching us. He removed his gun—a needle carbine—from his belt, flipped up the catch, took a cartridge and quietly slipped it into the gun. I fully understood the action; *my time had come.* I asked God to have mercy on my soul. I was ready. I think that no man fears to die when he knows that death is inevitable. I know that I did not, but the mental torture of the last twenty-four hours had made death welcome. Its near approach was a relief.

The chief took his gun in his hand, ready to raise it, and then looked me squarely in the eyes for perhaps two minutes; it seemed that long to me, at least. I returned his look without flinching. No white man would flinch at such a time. Not a motion was visible in the group by which we were surrounded; not a syllable was uttered. He raised the gun, dropped it, and said:

"ME NO KILL'M YOU."

Me go kill'm elk now." My life was spared. What did it? I know that he meant to kill me. Every motion and look, both of his and the surrounding Indians, convinced me of this. He said further:

" Me tell you no go. No try to get'm way. Injun kill'm, you go. Me tell you now, you stay with squaw. You lead'm mule. Me going to kill'm elk now. Me tell you, no go."

Pointing over the valley on the trail, I said:

" Me no go. You see'm white girls. Me stay with white girls. Me no go, *you bet.*"

Reader, this conversation may not interest you much, but to me it was the most intensely interesting little talk of my life. It has lost its charm; at least I do not care for a repetition.

It was at least three minutes before I could make myself believe that I was still alive. It took that long, if not longer, for my heart to leave my throat.

The chief took his snaky eyes from my face, and, saying something to the squaw, started off the trail to the timber. We again moved ahead, and as we rode along the Indians would point their fingers at me and say:

"Heap good, you. Heap squaw, you. Heap squaw.."

I took their gibes in good part, as I could not help myself.

As we rode along I saw many things that were supremely ludicrous, and they have been the cause of much merriment to Emma and myself since. I did not see anything very funny in it then. There is one thing though I cannot well forget. It was this:

About two miles from the scene, the particulars of which I have just related, we saw an Indian riding slowly along and trying to decorate himself with five yards of mosquito bar that he had stolen from our wagon. He would pass it over his shoulder, then around his waist, but there was more of it than he could manage. He would try it one way, then another, but with no satisfactory result. He was too fastidious. Again he would try, look at himself, and again remove it. It did not suit. Finally he stopped his horse, and sprang off with a motion that was the very essence of disgust, and, passing behind his horse, tied one end of it to the horse's tail. He viewed it with satisfaction. Mounting his horse he started ahead along the column as fast as he could go, with the mosquito bar streaming out behind. The Indians seemed to enjoy the sport, and as he passed they each gave him an encouraging shout. It was fun for the Indian but hard upon the horse.

As we rode along, the squaw I was with stopped her pony and got off to fix the pack on the kyuse she was leading, and climbed back on. She did this twice. The next time she made a move to dismount, I told her to sit still and I would fix the pack, and dismounted. This amused her considerably; I presume it was the first attention ever shown her. I arranged the pack, and politely raised my hat. She laughed outright. I remounted, and every time that the pack needed adjusting I would jump down and put it to rights, with the greatest politeness. I was more than polite.

I was dressed lightly, wearing nothing but a blue drilling blouse, light overalls and my underclothing, and as the wind arose on nearing the Yellowstone, I was uncomfortably cool. The wind continued to rise, and I grew correspondingly cooler. Looking around I saw a big greasy Indian with my overcoat comfortably buttoned about him. It made me mad. It was a good coat; a large blanket overcoat that I had slept in during the trip; but it wasn't the value of the coat that roiled me. It was the principle involved. As he rode up I said:

"Heap coat."

"Yes, heap coat. Heap warm," and he wrapped it more tightly around him. How I did want to reach out and snatch that Indian out of that coat. He, the dirty thief, riding along so comfortably in my coat, and I chilled through.

We soon could see the Yellowstone about a half mile below us. We soon passed Mud Geyser and the Devil's Well. Near the river we came to a group of Indians surrounding a white man. The Indian with my coat, said to me;

"Who white man?"

"I don't know," I answered.

"Come with me," he said, and we rode up to where they were.

"Hallo," says the white man, "are you a prisoner too?"

"Yes, are you?" I asked.

"No, the Indians turned me loose," he replied.

He then began telling me of the Helena party, another party of young men on their way to the geysers, who were encamped six or eight miles below, but I gave him a wink and he stopped. The Indian with me turned and asked me what I had said. I told him nothing. He then asked the other white man what I had said; he replied, nothing. The Indian now got pretty warm, and whirling around and facing me, angrily asked:

"What you tell him?"

"Nothing!" I said, about as loudly as he asked.

My squaw, so to speak, as I was her property, now said to me, "come," and I followed her. As we rode away I heard the white man say to the Indian that he was going, as White Bird had turned him loose, and told him to go home. The next I saw of him he was fording the river in charge of the Indian.

We crossed the river and found that the Indians were going into camp for noon near the fording. We were passing through the camp, when I saw Emma and Ida about seventy-five yards distant from us. The girls were looking forlorn. Ida happened to look up, and saw me. She jumped to her feet and ran towards me, hallooing.

"Frank, I want to see you, hold on. O Frank, I want to see you."

I told her to go back and I would see her soon. She had reached the side of my horse and kept begging for me to stop, but I was compelled to go on. I called for Emma to come out and take her back to camp, which she did.

We went on some distance farther when the squaw stopped, sprang from her pony and motioned me to do the same. I dismounted and removing the packs, turned the mule and horses loose.

The squaw then gave me a wooden pail and told me to go and get some water. I started for the river, about three hundred yards distant, and as I passed along the Indians raised their guns at me several times. I was more than nervous. On arriving at the river bank, I had to pass through a group of Indians standing there, but seeing no other chance to get down, pushed them aside and got the water. It was a delicate business for me, but they did not offer to molest me.

As I returned the Indians kept pointing at me and saying,

"heap squaw; heap squaw." I did not care so long as they only kept their tongues going. I could stand that.

Arriving at camp, the squaw asked me if I could cook.

"Yes," I replied.

"Cook'm bread," she said pointing to some flour and a pan.

I took the pan and put several cups flour in. Seeing some saleratus in a paper, I asked her if I should put some of that in, and she told me to do so. I put in about one and a half tablespoonfuls and began mixing it with the flour. I stirred away until she said:

"Make'm bread. Put'm in water. Make'm bread."

I put in some cold water and stirred it again, then added some hot water to make a pretty stiff dough. I then made up six round loaves and put them in an old frying pan in which I baked them, the squaw watching me closely all the time. The bread was soon baked, and it was a good rich color, that is if yellow is a rich color.

The squaw had not been sitting idle but had made some willow tea and fried a little bit of bacon. She then turned to the Indians and told them that dinner was ready. At least I supposed she did, as they came crowding around for their rations. They still kept pointing their fingers at me and saying, "heap squaw."

As they were about to sit down, an Indian came tearing over the hill and into camp at a fearful rate, shouting as he came. The Indians sprang to their feet and the camp was soon in the wildest commotion; Indians running here and there, shouting, getting up their ponies and starting on a run across the river. I got up beside a tree to see what was wrong, until I heard one Indian say "soldiers, soldiers." I would have given ten years of my life to have seen three or four hundred soldiers come marching over the hill then. Seeing that the Indians took the back trail on the other side of the river, and that the squaws remained in camp, I knew that the warriors were going to meet Howard's troops.

Soon the excitement subsided and I found that all the "bucks" had gone except seven or eight chiefs and about twenty-five warriors.

The squaws motioned for me to sit down and eat, which I did, eating sparringly of the bread and drinking a little of the tea.

About half an hour after we had eaten, our chief came back from his elk hunt. He rode up and says:

"Hello?"

I jumped up and pointing to the hind quarters of a deer which he had on his horse behind him, asked:

"Catch'm?"

"Yes, catch'm deer," he answered.

His squaw now came and took the meat, and turning to me, said:

"Cook'm more bread."

I went through the process of bread making, and the squaw placed the meat in a couple of pots and placed it on the fire. She let it remain about long enough to get it warmed through, when she removed it and the chief, another Indian, and herself sat down to eat. Then followed one of the greatest gastronomic feats I had ever witnessed. They ate the hind quarters of the deer, five loaves of bread, a half pan of cammas root, drank a camp kettle of tea, and quit hungry. I thought of Dingee. It was a meal that discounted his. I had heard that an Indian could eat enough at a meal to last him a week, and I think these could have eaten enough at one meal to last them a month. I have often wondered at the large appropriations made by the government for the support of these Indians, but if this was but an ordinary "feed," I do so no longer. The "whiskey-ring of Montana" are welcome to such solace as this gives.

The frugal repast being finished, the Indians heaped the pans and pots together, then sat around in different places eating dessert caught with a fine comb.

Soon I saw Shrively, Emma, and Ida coming over to our camp, and the events of the next half hour I pass over. I only pray that you, reader, may never have to endure what I did.

Shrively now came up to us from where he had been sitting,

and said the girls had better go back to camp, as Joe might be displeased with their long absence, and refuse to let them come again. My sisters clung to me, and with their arms about my neck begged me to kill them rather than leave them with the Indians. I was compelled to force them from me. Shrively promised me that they should never want for a friend, and that he would never leave them.

I have said that on first seeing Shrively as he stepped from the bushes into the trail in front of Houston and our party, that he was the worst looking specimen of humanity I ever saw. I thought now that he was the best looking man beneath the heavens. To me, he was glorified. You cannot imagine how relieved I felt to know that I should leave among these devils, at least one friend to my sisters.

They returned to White Bird's camp, and for the next two hours I did nothing but sit and watch the loungings, rather than motions of the Indians. They were spread around in the grass, some smoking and jabbering, and others with a portion of their clothing removed picking off desserters (not deserters) as aforesaid. This was the occupation of my chief and his squaw, they taking turns in combing, with astonishing results. I think I never read of a more degraded worthless set.

After a time my chief came near me, and I asked him if I could go down where the white girls were. He said, " yes; me go too; come."

As we approached the camp we saw a number of Indians sitting together, and near them were Shrively and the man that had been captured across the river that day by the overcoat thief. I nodded as I passed the group, and went on to where Emma and Ida were sitting on some robes a few paces beyond.

While sitting here we saw a number of squaws and papooses wearing coats, jackets and overcoats, belonging to our party Emma called my attention to a little Indian who was strutting around dressed in her sacque, wrong side in front, and nothing else. As he capered around among the others, he seemed to feel his superiority, and was in nowise diffident about showing it. We

THE GRAND CANYON, YELLOWSTONE VALLEY.

also saw a squaw wearing the skirt of Mrs. Cowan's riding habit. She had it fastened about the neck instead of the waist, and paraded with the stateliness of a Martha Washington.

In about half an hour after my arrival here, we saw Joe coming into camp. He came up to where we were and saluted us with a "hello," to which I responded, "hello, Joe." He picked up a papoose and held it arm's length for a minute, playing with it, then kissing it, sat it down. He turned to the Indians near him, said something that I did not understand, and then went to the middle of the camp and began haranguing the Indians as before.

He soon came back and motioned for Shrively and the other white man to get up, and he spread a blanket on the ground a little ways from where we were, and told them to sit down upon it. He spread another blanket for us to sit upon, and we sat down, wondering what all this meant. We were not long left in doubt. Our fates were to be determined by

A COUNCIL.

He now said something to the Indians, and a number of them sat down in a circle near us. I saw that there were seven of them, and that they were all chiefs. The other Indians near us stood around the circle as spectators.

Joe arose and, pointing to Emma, Ida and myself, addressed the other chiefs in broken English, saying:

"Send'm home. Send'm home to Bozeman. Send'm down river to Bozeman. No kill him, (pointing to me). No kill sisters. Send'm home to Bozeman. No kill." He sat down.

Emma and Ida began to cry, and I admit it was calculated to to make one nervous.

Little Bear now arose, and I could see at a glance that he was not a friend. I may have been prejudiced, but I thought him the worst looking Indian I ever saw. He was dressed in a complete suit of scarlet, trimmed with black. He wore a hood or cowl, and to me he seemed a devil incarnate. As he arose I could see hatred gleaming from his snake-like eyes, and as he proceeded to harangue the Indians he grew furious. When excited he was hideous. He spoke in substance as follows:

"Kill. Kill'm. No let'm go. White man bad. Kill'm him (pointing to me). Kill'm them (pointing to Shrively and the other prisoner). Kill'm all. White man no good. Citizen's kill'm my friends. Kill'm you friends. Kill'm squaw. Kill'm papoose. Kill'm friends in Big Hole fight. Heap kill Injun Big Hole fight. Citizens no good. Me tell you kill'm him (again pointing to me). Kill'm them (again pointing to the other men). Take'm white woman. Me take'm her (pointing to Emma). Make'm squaw. Take'm little white girl. By'm-bye make'm squaw too. Injun no let white man go. Heap kill."

He continued thus for some fifteen minutes, growing more excited as he spoke. His gestures and the manner of his pawing the ground when excited were terrible to witness, and I could see that his speech was having the desired effect upon the chiefs. They were getting excited and angry. Joe observed that he was gaining ground, and jumping to his feet, said:

"*No kill.* You sit down."

Little Bear sat down, though unwillingly, and Joe continued:

"No kill. Me send'm home. Him sisters no kill. Nez Perce no kill. Send'm home to Bozeman. Me tell you Nez Perce no kill. Me tell you now no kill. No kill'm white woman. No make'm squaw. Live twelve years in Montana. Everybody know'm white girls. Me tell you now no kill. Send'm home to Bozeman. Me tell you Nez Perce, you kill'm him, you make'm white girls squaw, citizens come, heap citizens come, catch'm Nez Perce, kill'm Nez Perce. Me tell you now no kill. Citizens come, kill'm Nez Perce. No stop kill'm Nez Perce. You kill him, make'm white girl squaw, me tell you citizens come, never stop kill'm Nez Perce. Never stop. Never stop kill'm Nez Perce. Send'm home. Send sisters to Bozeman. You kill, citizens come, never stop kill'm Nez Perce. Never stop kill'm Nez Perce."

Joe's speech helped our cause, yet on the faces of some of the chiefs we could see nothing but hatred. As they kept their eyes fixed on our faces, trying, it seemed, to read our thoughts, it was terrible.

As he sat down Joe took his pipe from a beautifully beaded buskin pouch, and began filling it with tobacco. During the time the Indians were talking in an undertone, but never removed their eyes from our faces.

Having filled the pipe he lighted it, and giving it a whiff or so, passed it to the chief sitting next on the left. This chief took it and gave it a whiff and passed it back. This was two votes for liberty. Joe gave the pipe another whiff, and passed it to the next chief on the left, who took it but passed it to the next without smoking. This was the first vote for death. The fourth chief raised it to his lips, took a long whiff and passed it back to Joe. Our hearts beat lighter, as this was the third vote for liberty. Joe again took a draw and passed it to the fifth man who passed it to Little Bear. This was two votes for death. Little Bear motioned it away with a spiteful gesture, and *the vote was a tie*, with one more to vote. Oh how we watched every motion of that Indian. Upon him—depended all. The girls were crying now, thinking, as I did, that it was a forlorn hope. I saw nothing in his countenance to betoken sympathy, yet I never watched anyone as I did him. He took the pipe, paused an instant as if playing with our misery, then placed it to his lips and gave a vigorous puff. *We were saved.* The suspense was so great that I think I was stunned by the suddenness of the announcement, and although the vote was taken twice more I realized but partially the transaction.

I think no one ever suffered more keenly than I did during the progress of this council. As the vote progressed the girls grew more frightened, and before it was concluded they were clinging to my neck and crying for me to kill them, rather than let the Indians get them. During the progress of the vote, Ida observed some squaws collecting wood for cooking purposes, and, supposing it was for the purpose of burning us, screamed:

"Frank, Frank, they are going to burn us alive. Kill me! Kill me! Don't let them burn us!"

My God, it was horrible. I could not wish the worst enemy I have on earth a tithe of the mental agony I endured during the time that the council lasted. I believe that I came as near going wild during that three-quarters of an hour as it is possible to do. I could see the tears trickling down the weather-beaten cheeks of Shrively at the agony of Emma and Ida. No amount of physical pain would bring a tear or a moan from such a man, yet he cried like a child at the sight of so much suffering of a woman. Inured to the hardships and vicissitudes of a mountaineer's life, he still had a heart as large as the mountains in which he lives.

FREEDOM.

The council being over the chiefs arose and, with the exception of Little Bear, who had gone off in disgust, had joined the crowd that had surrounded us during the exciting proceedings of the council. Joe came to us and said:

Send home now. Send'm your sisters home now. You three go home now."

Emma and I crossed ourselves and thanked him for our lives. He motioned us to get up, and I went to the chiefs, each in turn, and shook hands with all, thanking those who voted for us.

Joe told me to go and get a grey horse that stood about a hundred yards from us, and I took a rope, lassoed it, and soon brought it into camp. He said to me on my return:

"Your sisters ride, you walk," to which I assented, telling him I only wanted a chance to try my powers in that way. He said, further:

"No get'm saddle for little girl. She ride'm bareback. Me no get'm saddle."

He went out and soon returned with a yellow horse for Mrs. Cowan to ride and put an old saddle without stirrups upon it for her to ride in. He said he could not find her side saddle, but he found her riding skirt and waterproof and gave them to her. He also picked up a piece of bread and gave it to her, saying:

"Eat'm little. Drink'm water, no starve."

Shrively gave Emma the address of his relatives that she might write them of his fate in case he did not escape.

We were now ready to depart and bidding the old man an affectionate farewell, the girls mounted their horses. Joe now led up his horse, or rather Mrs. Cowan's horse, and taking his gun, bade me get on behind him. I did so, and we started for the river.

HOMEWARD BOUND.

Joe and I were in advance, Mrs. Cowan came next and Ida was in the rear. The river was high, and as we were nearing the shore I looked back to see if all was well, I saw Ida perched upon the withers of her horse as high as she could get and the water running over the horse's back. I believe she would have said nothing if she had drowned, such was her anxiety to get away. Seeing her perilous position, I said:

"Joe, see little white girl, quick!"

He turned his horse instantly, and started back to her, telling her to keep up the river farther. On reaching her I got the horse by the bridle and led it ashore.

Joe told me his troubles as we were crossing, and he also told why the Nez Perces had taken the trail.

Having reached the Mud Spring we stopped and Joe asked me if I had matches. I told him that we had not, and he gave me some. I dismounted and Emma and Ida joining us, Joe turned and said:

"Now my friends, good bye. You go down river, way down. No stop. Go all night. No stop. You go three days, get'm Bozeman. You go all night."

"No get'm Bozeman, Joe, in three days. One hundred and fifty miles, no get'm Bozeman," I replied.

"You no get'm Bozeman three days, Injun catch'm you," he again said.

"All right," I said, and being anxious to get away, I extended my hand and said:

"Good bye, Joe."

"Good bye, my friend," he replied, "good bye, my sister. Go now."

We had gone perhaps two hundred yards when we heard Joe coming after us with his horse at a gallop. Emma and Ida sprang from their horses and ran to where I was, saying, "we are gone now."

Joe rode near us and said:

"Hold on, my friends. Me want you to tell'm people in Bozeman me no fight no more now. Me no want to fight Montana citizens. Me no want to fight Montana soldiers. Me want peace. Me no want to fight no more now. You tell'm Bozeman people."

"Yes, me tell'm, Joe," I said. Pointing to the Nez Perces camp, I continued:

"Joe, red Indian out there bad Indian. Want'm my sister, make'm squaw. Joe, he come catch'm us by'm-bye. Bad Indian follow us down river, catch'm us."

"Red Injun, bad Injun. Him Snake, Little Bear no good. Him bad Injun. My friend, me stay here half hour, watch'm Snake Injun. Him cross river me kill'm. G—d d——n Snake Injun. No good. Watch'm him. Me watch'm Nez Perce, too. G—d d——d Nez Perce. Me tell'm no kill you friends. Me tell'm yesterday no kill you, you friends. —— Nez Perce. Me go way head, they go back, kill'm you friends. —— Nez Perce. Me no find out who kill'm you friend. Kill'm her husband. Me no find out who kill'm. —— Nez Perce. Me tell'm to-day no kill no more. Me want peace. No kill no more. Nez Perce kill'm any more, me shoot'm Nez Perce. —— Nez Perce. Me chief, tell'm Nez Perce, no kill no more. Me kill'm Nez Perce, they kill'm any more. —— Nez Perce!"

Joe got considerably worked during the delivery of this little address, and swore terribly. I doubted his sincerity, and know that he lied when he said he had told them not to kill me. He was evidently following a course dictated by policy, rather than principle. I had learned the lesson of distrust and it abides with me still. He continued:

"Good bye, my friends. Me tell you no go back towards

Henry's Lake. No go that way. Injun go back to fight Howard's soldiers. Gone back Henry's Lake."

I said to him:

"Joe, Indians gone down river to catch Helena party. Indians down there," pointing down the river.

"No Injuns down there," he replied, "catch'm Helena party long time ago. Injun got'm horse long time ago. No Injun down there. Now my friends, good bye."

We began to move off, when Joe again said:

"You tell'm people Bozeman me want peace. Me no want fight more. Me no want fight Montana citizens. No want fight Montana soldiers. No want fight no more. Me go to Shoshone country, but you tell people me kill Lewistown soldiers all time. No stop kill'm Lewistown soldiers. You tell'm."

"Yes, I tell'm, Joe."

"Tell'm in papers in Bozeman, me tell you."

"All right Joe, I tell'm."

"My friends, you tell'm Bozeman people me Poker Joe. Everybody know Poker Joe in Bozeman. Me *Hi'yu* chief now. Big chief me. Tell'm all people in Montana, tell'm all citizens in Montana, if they come fight me any more, me kill all time. No stop kill any more. Me kill, Nez Perce kill. Kill'm all time. Kill'm every body. White man, white woman, papoose. Kill'm all time. Never let'm go again, (pointing to us.) You tell'm. Now citizens come any more, soldiers come any more, me kill all time. Never stop. Good bye, my friends."

"Good bye, Joe. You set'm my sisters free. You set'm me free. Me thank you, Joe. Maybe sometime soldiers catch'm you, me save you maybe. Me try anyway."

"My friend," he replied, "soldiers never take'm me 'live, me die first. No take'm me 'live, me die first!"

"Don't know, Joe. They catch'm you some time, maybe. I help you then."

"Never catch'm me 'live," he said.

Again we exchanged the "good bye," and as I shook his hand I crossed myself. He turned to Mrs. Cowan, and said:

" Good bye, my sister."

" Good bye, Joe," she replied and made the sign of the cross.

Joe now turned to Ida and taking her hand, said:

" Good bye, my little sister."

Ida was crying, and as she bade him good bye she endeavored to make the sign as I had instructed her, but could only get half of it, that from the face to the breast, without crossing herself. This she did several times, noticing her mistake each time, and growing more confused the more she tried. It was pitiful to witness her distress, and yet it was ludicrous. She would say:

" Good bye, Joe, (motion) I—(motion) shall always— (motion) pray for— (motion) you, Joe, (motion.)

I could not help laughing, and I saw Emma smiling through her tears, It was the most complete "give way" I ever saw. Our catholicism was at an end.

Joe looked up and laughed outright as he saw the true state of affairs, but he good humoredly said:

" Good bye, my little sister, *you all right, any way!*" Turning to us, he said:

" Go quick now. Go quick!"

We took his advice, and for the next few miles we moved quickly.

We turned down the Yellowstone and ascended a high hill. Having reached the summit and being out of sight of the camp and Joe, we abandoned the trail and struck into the timber on the left and entered a group of pines about two hundred yards from the trail. We here stopped to listen, as Emma imagined that she heard some one following us. We could hear nothing.

From our position we could see down the Yellowstone some eight miles, and as it was all open country, we could see the course of the trail all that distance. To follow this would expose us to the view of the Indians, as the position of their camp was selected partly because it commanded a full view of this trail. To the south-west towards Henry's Lake, distant about sixty-five or seventy miles, we could see timber, and we knew that it extended unbroken all the way. Off to the left of Sulphur mountain, north-east from our position, distant three or four miles, we could see a mountain, not very high, with some scrubby pines on the summit.

I said to the girls that to reach that mountain was our only chance. Reaching it unobserved we could hide among the pines for the night. It is an open country lying between us and the mountain, and I knew that we had to do some fast traveling across it. I said to the girls:

" Girls we will, have to run for it. About a mile and a half from here we will strike a little creek that will shelter us from observation at the camp."

" I do not see the creek,' said Emma.

" You cannot see it until you strike it," I replied, "It is there nevertheless; and once there we are, for the time safe."

She said:

" It is all timber land between us and Henry's Lake. Let us go that way."

" No," I said, "we cannot get back that way. The Indians are back there, and we can never get through."

" I don't care," she replied, " I am going back where George is, I don't care if they do kill me. I am going to try and find him!"

" Emma, you can't go back. That's all there is about it. You would never get there. But if you did the Indians will get you sure."

" Frank, I do not care. You and Ida can go home. I am going to George. We can never get away from these Indians, anyway. I know they are following us. If we have to die, let us get back where George is. I do not care how soon they kill me after I get back to his body. I am going back."

" Emma, Cowan is dead. What good will it do to go back to him now? You can not help him, and there is no use in rushing back into the Indians' hands. They will not kill you, but you will be taken prisoner again and be a thousand times worse off than before. *You shall not go to Cowan!*"

I thought then, and still think, that even had I known that

Cowan was not dead, I acted judiciously. It seemed to me she was crazed by the events of the day before.

I seized the bridle, slipped the reins over the horse's head, and provided myself with a good stout club, and said further:

"You stay upon the horse; we have got to get out of this. Go with us to that mountain and then if you still insist on going back, I will go with you."

"All right," she said, "I will go that far."

I then led the horse out of the timber, and, handing her the reins, said:

"We will now have to run for it."

I took the horse by the tail, and, telling Ida to keep up, I brought the horse a whack with the club that started him at the top of his speed. I hung on to the tail, and every jump the horse made I gave him a whack. We made excellent time for that mile and a half. Had Joe seen us, he would have thought that we had followed his advice to the letter.

We reached the creek that winds down through the open country among low bluffs, that were not visible from our position among the pines, and here I told Emma to stop, while I went back to see if we had been observed from camp and followed. I crept to the top of a knoll but could see no signs of Indians, and returned.

We turned down the creek and went, perhaps, a half mile and struck another small creek that I had rightly guessed was tributary to this, and that headed up near the mountain that we wished to reach. We turned up the creek and found that its banks would effectually conceal us from the Indians in camp. We forced our horses ahead at as lively a gait as the nature of the ground would permit, and by a mile's travel we reached the foot of the mountains.

In ascending the mountain was our greatest danger, since the Indians would certainly see us if they were looking in that direction, as the mountain's sides were bare and in plain view of the camp.

Telling the girls to remain where they were, I again went back to a little knoll from which to reconnoiter. I saw some Indians skirting the timber land, going towards the Geyser Basins, but they soon disappeared, and I returned to the girls.

I helped Emma upon her horse, she having dismounted, and again laid hold of the friendly tail of the horse. We had about three-fourths of a mile to make the summit, and I presume that the same distance on a mountain, going up, was never passed over quicker. I used my persuader, the club, in a manner anything but pleasant to the horse.

It was near sun-down now, and I concluded we had better camp for the night. I tied the horses to a sappling, leaving them fixed in such a way, with their saddles on, that should any one find them they would suppose we had abandoned them and taken to the timber on foot.

The girls had got wet in crossing the river, and, as the sun went down they began to get very cold, I thought it would be perfectly safe to build a fire, and, with that intention, scooped out a hole in the loose earth and placed some dry leaves and grass in it for that purpose. As I touched a match to it, the blaze shot three or four feet above the surface, and Ida immediately dashed upon it the earth I had removed, putting it out, saying she would rather freeze to death than be re-captured by the Indians. Emma also said she wanted no fire, and, telling them to remain where they were, I took a scout around the mountain for Indians.

In looking around I found a place where two trees, in falling, had crossed, and beneath them was a place that afforded both a shelter and a hiding place. I returned to the girls and, telling of my good fortune, we took the horse blanket Joe had given us, and proceeded to the trees. The girls crawled beneath them, and, covering them as best I could with the blanket, I again returned to the summit to keep watch during the night.

The moon was now up, and its bright light made objects at a distance quite distinct. As I looked off towards the Geyser Basins, I saw objects moving on the trail from the basins to the river, which I took to be Indians. They disappeared after a time, and seeing nothing more, about midnight I returned to the girls.

I found them complaining of the cold, but they would not consent to my making a fire, so I crept in beside them and tried to keep them warm. We simply suffered till daylight.

At the first signs of day we left our place of concealment, when I found that the girls were so benumbed with the cold that they could scarcely walk. After walking about for some time they regained the use of their limbs, and we were again ready for the trail. Mrs. Cowan had concluded to follow my advice, and consented to our following the river towards Bozeman.

We went to our horses, and, removing their bridles, let them graze for a time, and again mounted them for our homeward trip.

We descended the north side of the mountain, forded Alum Creek at its base, and then hurried across the open country beyond, to the timber, three or four miles distant on the mountain side, which we reached, just as the sun was coming up. We entered the timber some thirty or forty yards, so as not to be visible from the camp, and traveled thus, skirting it, until we struck the trail leading to the falls of the Yellowstone, some three or four miles below, and about eight miles from where we parted company with Joe.

As we struck the trail I saw a number of fresh pony tracks, and told the girls that the Indians were below or in advance of us. Emma wished to abandon the horses, and take to the timber on foot. We stopped to determine what to do, and as we were conversing, Ida exclaimed:

"What is that?"

We could hear nothing for a time, but directly heard what seemed to be some one chopping in the distance. Emma was sure it was the Indians below us, but I thought not, and proposed that we move forward a little ways, and gain a position where we could see down upon the river. We advanced cautiously, still hearing the sound at intervals as we proceeded. We reached a point where we could look down upon the river, but could see nothing that would indicate the presence of human beings, either friend or foe. We were intently listening when a wood-pecker flew upon a tree near us and began pecking a dry bough, producing the same sound that we had heard. I remarked that that was the noise, and proposed that we now push ahead as rapidly as discretion would permit. Ida, however, insisted that it was not that kind of noise, and I am now convinced that she was right, as we afterwards learned that Joe had lied to us about the capture of the Helena party the day before, and that they were captured about noon on the day we heard the noise, (Sunday), at a point on the river just below where we were. They were within a short distance of us, and were separated from us only by a small hill. Had we only found them we would have been spared much suffering, and saved the lives of those of the party that were here murdered in a few hours afterwards.

I now told the girls that I would go in advance a short distance and thus be on a look out for Indians. I instructed them to immediately abandon the horses and strike into the timber in case I gave them warning of approaching danger, and that I would try to stand the Indians off until they made good their escape.

We proceeded thus for a mile or so, when we again found fresh pony tracks. I supposed from the number that there must have been twenty ponies. We came to a place that was tramped over as if there had been a scuffle here, and Emma suggested that it must have been the scene of the capture of the Helena boys. I think now, that it was where the ponies had been hitched the night before. Here I found a red scarf that I supposed had been dropped by one of the boys, but on smelling it I found that it was most assuredly the property of an Indian. There is no mistaking the smell.

A little further on we came to where the trails separated, one bearing to the right, leading, as Houston told us, down by the Upper Fall, and the other, being that which we had taken to the Lower Fall. We took the right hand trail, and I soon saw that the Indians had taken the left. I felt then that we were safe from immediate capture, at least.

I was now greatly fatigued and ravenously hungry, and it occurred to me to try an experiment that I had often heard was the means by which the Indians could endure so much fatigue and hunger. I took the scarf, and using it as a belt, drew it tightly about me. I felt much lighter, and the pangs of hunger less. During the day, I would occasionally tighten it, and, whether there be any virtue in it or not, I know it helped me greatly.

We now ascended the mountain near the Lower Falls, and passing a little to the left, we could hear them roaring. I wanted Emma to stop and see the falls, but she peremptorily refused. Ida also wished to go ahead as speedily as possible, and we proceeded onwards. Attaining the summit, we crossed a little valley lying between the foot of Mt. Washburn and the Lower Falls. Here we found the camp of the Helena boys when they had visited the falls. We could see the tent-pegs where they had pitched their tents.

Soon after passing this we came to more pony tracks. We halted and upon examination I found the marks of a trailing rope. I said to the girls that this was Texas Jack's party and that they were not far in advance. This gave us new courage, and we pushed ahead more briskly than before and soon passed over the four miles of flat lying between us and Mt. Washburn.

We began the ascent of the mountain about eight o'clock and we did not reach the summit until about one o'clock. I never undertook a more difficult ascent, and weakened as we were, with fasting and want of rest, it was almost impossible for us to reach the summit. It was the most tiring task that I ever performed.

As we reached the summit, Ida exclaimed:

"Oh, I am so tired!"

This was the first complaint from any member of the party, and I know she was suffering or she would not have given up. One of her age must have felt more keenly the pangs of hunger, than did we. Telling her to wait until we got down the mountain, we took an observation of the surrounding country before beginning the descent. We could see miles in every direction, but the prospect only discouraged us; we could see at a glance, the many obstacles to be encountered in our advance. Nothing but mountains, ragged cliffs and dense timber on every hand.

The air on Mt. Washburn was extremely cold as we were surrounded by snow and we soon began our descent. We went about a half mile below the snow limit, and camped off the side of the trail in some pines, and unbridled our horses and turned them loose to graze.

Emma was impatient to go ahead and get beyond the possibility of recapture, and notwithstanding the fact of my showing her that we were in greater danger from those in advance, than from those in the rear, she insisted on our going on as speedily as possible. We did not let the horses eat long, although the jaded brutes needed it badly enough, and soon were on the road again.

The descent, although not so fatiguing, was a more dangerous one, as the trail wound in and out among the rocks, now up, then down, over rocks with fearful chasms, and by the edge of precipices that would make one shudder to glance over. We could still occasionally see the mark of the rope, and it was a constant source of encouragement, as I was momentarily expecting to see Jack's party. How eagerly I watched and listened!

After traveling for an hour or so, we again came in sight of the river, and looking back towards Mt. Washburn, which we had now left, and off to the right of the trail, I could see falls coming from the snow and falling hundreds of feet. They looked like bands of silver. I called Emma's attention to them, and looking at them for a moment, she said:

"Frank, I saw those falls from the Mammoth Hot Springs when father, mother, Ida, and myself were there four years ago. They are the Tower Creek Falls. We can not be far from the Springs now. Let us hurry on and we will find help there, as McCarty and McQuirk live there. We can get there before night, if we hurry."

We began the descent towards Tower Creek and could now see the Yellowstone quite plainly. At three P. M. we made the creek and here camped upon the camping ground of all tourists on their way to the geysers from Bozeman. It is the ground for the first night's camp after leaving the Springs.

We concluded to rest here for a time, and let our horses feed. Ida kept saying she was hungry. Emma had given her all the bread that she had, and we could do nothing more for her. I proposed, however, that we search among the remains of the camp fires, a great many of which are here found. We began the search by poking around in the ashes and kicking them aside, each hunting in a different direction from the other.

I found a piece of "hard-tack" and removed the dirt from it, and kept it until the girls came back. Emma soon returned, and I offered it to her but she declined it, saying she had found a piece of bread. Ida had not returned yet, and looking up the creek I saw her standing in a little thicket of bushes, partially concealed from view. I thought she acted strangely and called to her, saying:

"Ida, what are you doing?"

"Nothing," she replied.

But she made no move towards rejoining us, and stood with her hands behind her. Again I called:

"Why do you stand there? Come down here. What ails you?"

"Nothing," she again replied.

"Look here," I said, "Emma and I have found some bread!"

"I got a little piece too," she replied, "*I'm so hungry!*"

"Well, eat it, we do not want it."

She rejoined us, and showed us her treasure. It was a small piece, and seemed as if it might have been baked by Lewis and Clarke in '45.

The girls insisted on my eating the cracker that I had found, as I was subjected to greater exertions than they, being compelled to walk while they could ride. We ate what we had each found, and I think that I have never eaten anything that I relished so much. We had eaten nothing, comparatively, since Thursday night, the night prior to our capture. The want of rest was telling fearfully upon us, too; we had slept none since our capture.

After we had eaten our morsels of bread, we drank from the creek and felt much better and stronger. We were sitting beneath a large pine tree, and upon looking above our heads I saw the name of Richard Detrich, with the date August 25th. The Helena party had evidently camped here on Thursday night, the 24th, and this was written by Detrich on Friday morning, the 25th. I took a notice that was also posted here, and wrote upon the reverse our names with the statement that we were all that were left of a party of ten, captured on the 25th in the basin, with the date Aug. 27.

We got up the horses, crossed the creek and again began climbing mountains. The mountain just here was so steep, that the girls were compelled to dismount and walk up, holding to the horses tails and thus compelling them to pull them up. This had been my mode of traveling up the mountains.

After ascending this mountain we encountered nothing of note until we had reached a point about fifteen or sixteen miles from where we had camped, or rested rather. I was walking in advance as I had been doing throughout the day, except when climbing mountains, when I suddenly saw some distance in advance several head of horses grazing upon the mountain side.

"Look out! Indians," I said to the girls, who sprang from their horses and concealed themselves in the undergrowth of timber. Telling them to remain where they were, I cautiously advanced to reconoiter the position of the Indians.

Crawling upon my hands and knees I reached the edge of the hill and came to a place that gave me an unobstructed view up and down the creek, but I could see nothing of Indians. As I looked I saw smoke curling up above a clump of bushes beyond the creek. I watched it closely for a while, and directly saw a soldier rise. Thinking that he might be a captive, I still waited and soon had the inexpressible pleasure of seeing another rise. I knew then that we had found friends.

WE WERE SAFE.

I rushed back to where the girls lay concealed and shouted: "Come on, we are safe! They are soldiers!"

The girls sprang to their feet and fairly jumped for joy. I started on a run down the hill, leaving the girls to follow on the horses, and created no little sensation in camp as I sprang in among the soldiers with the heartiest, "How are you, Lieutenant?" that I ever uttered.

It was Lieut. Schofield with a squad of soldiers on a scout.

"How are you, sir?" he replied, as he examined me critically from head to foot.

"Got anything to eat?" I asked.

"Yes, who are those ladies coming down the hill?"

"Mrs. George Cowan, and Ida Carpenter, my sisters."

"What are you doing out here with them without grub?"

"We are all that is left out of a party of ten. But give us something to eat and I'll talk with you then."

The soldier boys began to bustle around lively and prepare supper for us. The girls came in to camp, and being introduced to the Lieutenant, asked for soap and a towel. The articles being supplied them, they went to the creek and washed, and said they felt much better. They certainly looked better. In the meantime I gave the Lieutenant an outline of our experiences with Chief Joseph's band, and such information as to their whereabouts, numbers, etc., as I could.

One of the boys took the horses and led them out to graze. As he removed the saddle from Emma's horse, he threw a deer's shank upon the ground with the remark "I guess you will not want that now." It was a bone that I had picked up on the way and tied upon the saddle, intending to make it the last resort before starvation. I thought I could make a soup from it, in a tin cup that I had found on the way, that had been dropped, probably by Texas Jack's party, and flattened out by a poney tramping upon it.

Supper was announced, and if I ever enjoyed eating I did then. Schofield said it did him good to watch us. It may be remarked that we did not stand on formality, neither do I remember that either of us crossed ourselves. I thought of Dingee and his melodious "grub pile." Poor fellow! I regretted the gibes I had given him in a spirit of fun.

11

emerged from the canyon and, crossing the river, were soon at the springs and

WITH FRIENDS.

Here we found Texas Jack's party. McCarty and all the rest did all for us that it was possible for them to do. About eleven o'clock Schofield came in and asked us if we wished to send any word to our friends, as he was going to send a courier to Bozeman that night. I sent a message for my brother in Helena to be telegraphed from Bozeman, telling him of the safety of Emma, Ida, and myself, but of the death, as I supposed, of the rest of the party. We soon retired to the rest that we all so much needed.

About three A. M. we were awakened by the tramp of horses and some one without hallooed, "Roll out, and let us in."

We sprang from our beds and on opening the doors found four of the Helena boys, Wilkie, Andy Weikart, Jack Stuart and the darkey, Ben. Stone. We took them in and found that two of them were badly wounded. Weikart was shot through the shoulder, a flesh wound, and Stuart had a bad wound in the ankle and another in the thigh, the ball having passed directly through it shattering the bone in its passage. We did the best we could for all, and dressed the wounds of the wounded men and made them as comfortable as we could. As a matter of course we slept no more that night.

The next morning Calfe and Catlin, two photographers, came and told us that if we would wait until ten o'clock they would take us to Bozeman with their four mule team. This was good news, as neither Emma nor Ida could walk or ride horseback.

Lieut. Schofield and soldier boys and Pfister, started for Bozeman early in the morning, and about ten o'clock we left the springs with Calfe and Catlin.

When we had reached the summit of the hill below the springs we saw Texas Jack looking through his spy-glass up the canyon towards Gardiner's River. Looking in the direction I saw two person running towards us in and out of the bushes skirting the river.

"Who is it?" I asked, "Indians or white men?"

" I think it is two white men," he replied, "but I think there are five or six Indians following them."

We afterwards learned that the two men were Detrich and Duncan.

Jack, turning to us, said:

" You go on and overtake our party which is not far in advance, and I'll go back and give those Indians a shot or two."

We now started down the mountain towards the Yellowstone three miles distant. Just as we began the descent we heard firing in the rear. This frightened Emma and Ida, and they became very nervous again. Calfe rode up behind us saying:

"Drive fast, Catlin, I guess the Indians have attacked the Springs."

Down the mountains we went pell mell, and we soon reached Henderson's Ranche, eight miles from the springs. Here we were rejoined by Texas Jack, who told us that he had shot two of the Indian ponies and driven the Indians back. This news relieved our anxiety considerably and we began to breath easier. We soon drove down into the canyon of the Yellowstone, a wild and rugged place, just suited for an ambuscade for Indians. We feared trouble here, but Texas Jack went in advance scouting for us, and about midnight we emerged on to Bottler's Ranche. The Bottler Brothers showed us every possible attention, and an old Scotch lady was very kind.

The next morning many friends from Emigrant Gulch and the surrounding country came in, and the ladies cheered up Mrs. Cowan considerably. Ide had fully recovered the use of her feet and here Texas Jack presented her with a pair of beautiful moccasins. They were very acceptable.

We remained here until about noon and then again took the road for Bozeman. We had not been gone more than an hour when we met Mr. David Boreum, of Bozeman, coming to meet us with a carriage. He is an intimate friend of Cowan's and having heard of this disaster that had befallen our party, immediately started to meet us. The sight of him awoke the pleasant mem-

and going in every direction. I saw two of the boys coming towards me and I lit out for the river. I reached the river and on looking back heard two shots and some one exclaim, "O, my God?"

I don't know who these two were but think it was Jack Stuart and Kenk. I swam the river, came down to Burnett's bridge, recrossed to this side, and here I am, and I am going to leave this section of country as soon as God Almighty will let me. I don't think any of the boys got away. The Indians piled the bullets in plenty."

Lieutenant Schofield told his boys to pack up and we would go to the springs that night, as the Indians were likely to visit us here at any time. He told Pfister and myself that he would give us a mule to ride down. Pfister said he would go ahead and we could overtake him, but I told him to hold on and we could ride the mule together. He agreed to this and after having disposed of his coffee and bacon, given by the soldiers, we were all ready to start.

Schofield said he had been on a scout to the top of Mt. Washburn but could see no Indians, but his guests were willing to testify that they were there nevertheless. I knew I not only heard, saw and felt them, but had tasted and smelt them as well. My five senses didn't deceive me.

We were soon mounted and off for the springs, distant eighteen or twenty miles, and began climbing over mountains again, and as Pfister and I rode along both on one mule, I gave him an account of the fate of our party.

We reached the canyon of Gardiner's River above the springs about nine o'clock that night, and then followed the passage of the canyon, a most difficult feat even in the broad light of day. The trail, which is very narrow, winds down through the canyon on the verge of a precipice hundreds of feet high. We could hear the roaring of the river in the rapids below us, but could see nothing as it was very dark, the moon not having risen. A misstep would have hurled us to instant death on the rocks below, and we cautiously threaded our way for an hour, when we

HOT SPRINGS, ON GARDINER'S RIVER.

Having satisfied the cravings of the inner man, I took an inventory of dry goods and clothing we had on hand. We were in a sorry plight, and I was forced to the conclusion that as true representatives of the Carpenter family, we were not a success.

Ida was bare-headed, bare-footed, with her dress torn to shreds. Emma was not much better, but she had the advantage of a hat. They were covered with dust, tanned, with eyes badly swollen from crying, and presented anything but a prepossessing appearance. It may have been a brother's prejudice, but I thought I had seen them looking better.

My clothing was scarcely worthy of note; that is, there was scarcely enough of it to note. It was a picturesque costume, though cool. I had been playing in a sanctimonious game since my capture, but that was not the exact reason for my *holy* suit. The hat Mann had given me, I "swapped off" to an Indian, and got a good one. It had not suffered any since our escape and was good yet, barring the loss of the crown and most of the rim. It rested tranquilly on my neck, while my head stuck through the top, and my ears through the sides, and what there was of the rim flapped cunningly up and down as I walked.

Lieutenant Schofield and his boys did all they could to relieve our wants, and furnished us with such clothing as they could. Among other things they gave Ida a soldier's overcoat which she wore gracefully.

We had been in camp but about an hour when the Lieutenant, looking up the trail, said:

"There comes another of your party down the hill now."

I jumped to my feet, and looking at the approaching person, said:

"That is none of our party. I guess it is one of the Helena boys."

All eyes were fixed upon the stranger now, who came tearing down the hill with his hat in his hand. He crossed the creek and came into camp and saluted us with a:

"Hello, Frank, is that you?"

"Yes, what's the matter?" I answered, "are you one of the Helena party?"

"Yes, and my name is Pfister. I guess the Indians got the rest of the boys."

"Where were you attacked?" asked Schofield.

"Just above the falls, to-day," he replied.

The little ripple of excitement caused by Pfister's summary entrance soon subsided, and he gave an account of the capture of the boys, about as follows:

"Our party consisted of Messrs., Kenk, Stuart, Roberts, Foller, Weikart, Duncan, Detrich, Wilkie, Ben. Stone, the colored cook, and myself, and were on our way to visit the Geyser Basins. Yesterday we were encamped near Sulphur Mountain, and during the afternoon one of the boys said he had seen either an herd of buffalo or elk, or a band of Indians, about five or six miles above us on the other side of the Yellowstone River. Duncan took a spy-glass and went up on the mountain to determine if possible, what they were. He soon returned and said they were Indians, and proposed that we get out of that as soon as possible. We, accordingly packed up and moved back three or four miles, when one of the boys proposed that we go no farther, as Howard was after the Indians, and by to-morrow they would be gone, and we pitched our tents there. We camped for the night, but some of the boys wanted to go back home, but the majority was of the mind to go ahead to the geysers, as we had come thus far, and the journey was almost completed.

Kenk and Duncan said they were going back, Indians or no Indians, and Kenk left us and went as far as the falls, but returned about ten o'clock last night, as no one had followed his example.

We got up about six or seven o'clock this morning, and Andy Weikart and Wilkie took their horses and went out on a scout. They were to fire their guns if they saw Indians, and we waited three or four hours for them to return. It was nearing dinner time and I left the camp for the purpose of getting wood, leaving some of the boys asleep, and the remainder sitting about the camp fire. I was busy getting wood when all of a sudden, pop, pop, went the guns and I heard the Indians' yip, yip! I looked around and saw the camp full of Indians with the boys jumping ories of the past and gave poignancy to Mrs. Cowan's grief.

We now bade Catlin and Calfe good bye, with warm thanks for their kindnesses, and transferred ourselves to the carriage of Mr. Boreum. Our baggage having been left in charge of Chief Joseph, we had no Saratoga trunks to bother us.

A drive of fifteen miles brought us to a ranche, where we stopped for supper. Here, we found quite a number of ladies who showed the girls every attention. By the time we had got supper it was late, and as the ladies had insisted on our remaining, we concluded to put up for the night. We retired about eleven o'clock, but not to sleep. I was nervous and lay awake for some time, but about one o'clock and was just falling asleep when I heard the tinkle of a bell and the tramp of horses coming up the valley. I knew instantly the meaning of it, and sprang up and said to Boreum, with whom I was sleeping:

"Dave, Indians! They are stampeding the horses in the valley."

Boreum was out instantly, and grabbing his gun and giving me a revolver, we started to bring in our horses. As we stepped out of the house we saw the flash and heard the report of two guns three or four hundred yards down the valley. The Indians had secured the horses, and were stampeding close to where the shots were fired.

We soon brought up the two carriage horses, and having tied them near us awaited further developments. Soon Calfe and Catlin came up with their team and told us that they had shot at the Indians when they were trying to cut the picket ropes of the mules.

Neighbors soon began coming in, and everything was for a time, in an uproar. The night was cloudy and dark, and we did not know what minute we might be attacked. Emma and Ida sprang from their beds at the reports of the guns, and were considerably frightened, and the crying of the neighbors as they came in was not calculated to allay their fears much.

It was not a time for merriment, yet I was amused at one incident. A fellow came running up to the house as rapidly as he could, and as he came to the door, he hallooed:

"Get up, get up! For God's sake, get up! The Indians are all around us and we will all be murdered before morning!"

Dave sprang out of the house and grasping the horse's bridle, and laying hold of the fellow, said:

"Here you d—d fool you, what ails you? Don't you know anything? There are two ladies in the house that have just got away from the Indians and they have gone through enough without your scaring them. Shut up your mouth you d—d fool you, or I'll blow the top of your head off!"

The fellow, who was almost frightened to death before, now seemed to be stricken dumb. He slid down off his horse and set down as meek as a lamb. It was the most sensible thing he could have done as Dave is in the habit of putting his threats into disagreeable execution. He is little, but he is large with a revolver.

The following morning the scene about the ranche was rather rumpled. It seemed as if every body in the country, with all their movable property had assembled here during the night. There were horses, packs, saddles, household goods, from a stove poker up, women, children, wagons, etc., etc., piled around promiscuously. In their disposition effect had not been studied but it was, nevertheless, pleasing.

We discovered that the Indians had not got away with any of the horses, as the shots of Calfe and Catlin had scared them off and they had abandoned everything and cut for the mountains.

At nine o'clock we were again *en route*, and we drove into Bozeman about noon, on Wednesday.

HOME AT LAST.

Ida, I presume, was the only member of the party that seemed to fully realize the pleasure of being among friends, free from danger again. Emma felt more keenly than ever her loneliness as all the surroundings constantly reminded her of Cowan.

As for myself, I not only mourned the loss of so many brave

"wipe off his chin, and give the boys the story," he began.

"Houston.—"Well, I came down from Clark's fork on Wednesday and heard at the springs of the shooting of Cowan and his party and the escape of Frank and his sisters. I inquired where it was, and they told me near the Mud Springs, and I started out to bury Cowan, and to try and find the balance of the party. I got up as far as Burnett's bridge where I found that 'cuss' (pointing to Jimmy) prowling around. He says, 'Hello, what's the matter with you?' and I replied 'I had lost some Indians and was going up the river to find them.'"

Jimmy (breaking in).—"Yes, and he found them, too. You'd a thought so to have seen him run."

Houston.—"Jim, shut your trap. Well, says Jimmy, I'll go with you. I then told him about Cowan and crowd. We got up skulking around all day Thursday, and on Friday afternoon we rode up on the top of a hill near Mud Geyser, when looking across the river I saw the squaw camp. Turning around to Jim, I said: 'we've struck it.' 'Struck what?' he asked. 'The squaw camp,' I replied."

Jimmy D. (again interrupting)—"Yes, and don't you think that cuss got off his horse and sat down there right in sight of camp."

Houston.—"Jim, who's telling this story, you or I? Well, I looked across the river and saw a white man and several Indians dressed in white men's clothing. 'Well,' says Jimmy, 'what you going to do about it?' I handed him the glass, and said, 'Let's take a trip through camp. We can cross the river, and get into the squaw camp, shoot what Indians we can, and pass through the camp up towards Clark's Fork. We can go through on a run, and they haven't anything that can catch us.'"

Jimmy D. (again)—"Yes, that d——d fool wanted to do that."

Houston.—"Well, I noticed that you said all right, you'd go if I would."

Jimmy D.—"Well, *I* noticed that we got up and went, too, but not across the river."

Houston.—"Well, we got upon our horses and d——d if we

weren't *surrounded by Indians.* Jim says, 'well, are these the Indians you lost, George?' I said, 'you just follow me,' and I turned Johnny (his horse) loose, and we made a break through them. They piled it to us lively, but didn't catch nary one of us. Then we had the prettiest race from there to the timber above the falls (eight miles) you ever saw."

Jimmy.—" I never saw a man run so fast since God made little apples."

Houston—"Well I notice that you kept so close to me that you didn't get any sand in your eyes. Well, we struck the timber and waited for the Indians to come up, but they took care not to come in rifle shot of the timber. They went into the grass plenty. We came down to Burnett's Bridge last night, saw some Indians crossing, camped in the hills, came in this morning and here we are."

On Sunday scouts were sent out again. Two scouts sent out on Saturday did not return until Sunday noon. They brought in two men that had received close calls. as one was shot through the neck, and the other had holes shot through his clothing. They were scouts from Sturgess' command with dispatches for Howard. One of the scouts, John Goff by name, had an Indian boy, that he had raised, with him when they met the Indians. The boy was killed and left near Burnett's Bridge.

I had become impatient at the delay, and on Monday morning asked Lieutenant Doane if he was going to move forward soon. He replied that he could not until he got orders to that effect. He added that he did not expect to go to the Lower Basin at all, as he thought his orders would be to follow the Indians. I told him then that I thought of returning to Bozeman, and trying to reach the basin by the route up the Madison. He thought it best for me to do so, as he could do nothing for me, and the party of citizens was too small to go ahead.

Houston advised me to return to Bozeman, and see the friends of our party, and he assured me he would find Cowan's body, and bury it. I concluded to follow the advice, and with Weikart,

"I seed de Injuns comin' aroun' in de foah-noon dis mornin'. I tole Detrich we had better be a gettin' out of dis, but he kept a sayin' 'I'll nebcr go back to Mrs. Roberts widout Joe.' 'Bout 'leven or twelve o'clock Detrich says, 'I'll go down an' change de hosses, repicket dem, while you git dinnah, Ben.' I say 'all right.'

"Well, while he was gone a changin' ob de hosses, I looked out ob de doah an' seed a Injun stick his head up ober a rock out in front ob de house. I didn't wait for no lebe, I didn't, an' dropped eberyting an' bolted trew de back doah, I did, up into de timbah an' laid down awaitin' for somethin' to do next. I seed de Injuns all 'bout de house an' pears like dey was mighty anxious to fine me, but I wasen't anxious to fine dem. It war gettin' along towards night, and I clim a tree. Purty soon a big Injun rode right down under de tree a searchin' aroun' for me. I jes hel' my bref an' say to myself, 'O Mr. Injun; good Mr. Injun, *don't look up dis way!*' Boys, I 'clare to goodness I could hab touched dat Injun's head wif my foot—— *but I didn't!*

"Bye'm-by de Injun go away down towards de springs an' I got down on to de groun' an' strike for de side ob de mountain whar I laid down. I was a layin' in de brush, when all ob a sudden I heerd a crackin in de brush. Den, boys, I got right down on my knees and prayed, (an' I hope de God A'mighty forgive me, I neber prayed before sense I lef' my modder's knee,) but I jes got down an' say 'O Lod God A'mighty, jes help me out ob dis scrape an' I will neber interfere wid you no moah!' I heerd dis noise an' a crashin' in de bushes again, and I jes laid down wid my face to de groun' an I spected to feel de tom hawk in de back of my head. All ob a sudden I turned ober and dar I seed a big black bar a lookin' at me. Boys, *I nebber was so glad to see a bar afore in my all life.* De bar he got up an' run, an' I got up an' rund to de top ob de mountain when I saw youah camp fire an' heah I is— bress de Lod!"

Weikart and McCarty arrived during the night and reported the burying of Kenk, and narrated their adventures. On their return they met the Indians that burned the ranche and had had their horses shot from under them. The details of their escape were interesting, but too long to be inserted here.

McCarty said that George Houston had been down to the springs on Wednesday and he and Jimmy Dewings had gone back to bury Cowan and the rest of our party.

Saturday morning a courier came from Bozeman with dispatches and orders for Lieut. Doane to remain where he was, and wait for Col. Gilbert and command. Doane now sent out his scouts and several couriers with dispatches to Gen. Howard. I sent a dispatch to Gen. Howard requesting to be informed of the recovery of any of the bodies of the party should they find them.

The different scouting parties came in Saturday night, some on foot, their horses having been shot from under them, and they barely escaping with their lives. They reported Indians all around us on the mountains. During the day a number of us went up to the springs and buried Detrich. Saturday night, stragglers from surrounding ranches kept coming into Doane's camp, and on Sunday morning Geo. Houston and Jimmy Dewings came into camp on a run with their horses wet with sweat. They were given something to eat and between bites Doane elicited the following:

Doane.—" Did you find the squaw camp?"

Houston.—" O, no, *we just found* the squaw camp.

Doane.—"How many Indians did you see?"

Houston.—" Plenty, you bet, they hooped us up lively, too!"

Doane.—"How are the Indians fixed as regards ammunition?"

Jimmy D.—G—d, they're fixed plenty, you bet your boots! Come d—n near fixing us. My Caeser, I never saw a man run so in all my life as George Houston did!"

" Houston.—" Well, I noticed that you kept up to me pretty well."

One of the crowd.—" George, go on and tell us all about it."

Jimmy D.—" Just wait till he gets through that pile of grub before him. He's got a government contract on storage."

Houston finished eating, and with a prompt from Jimmy to

boys and intimate friends, but I was constantly upbraiding myself for having induced them to go. True, they went voluntarily, yet I had organized the party and could not rid myself of the feeling that I was in a measure responsible for the disaster. It was I that proposed going to the Indians in opposition to the advice of Arnold, which perhaps, was the better and should have been followed. The fact, too, of none of them escaping with the exception of my own family, would appear against me in public opinion I thought, and added to my dissatisfaction with myself. Matters looked dark for me. I concluded there and then, that if none of the boys got out safe, Helena would see me no more.

Just as we were driving into Bozeman, we met Lieut. Doane with ninety-five Crow Indians on the way to catch Nez Perces. I remarked that, notwithstanding the saying "set a thief to catch a thief," I would bet he could not get one of his Crows to touch a Nez Perces. Subsequent events proved that I was right.

In Bozeman we went to the North Pacific Hotel, and were hospitably entertained by the gentlemanly proprietor, George Wakefield and his estimable lady, to whom we shall always entertain most grateful feelings.

We found that a party of citizens were being organized to go and bury Cowan and search for the bodies of the rest of the boys, and I asked Dave Boreum to provide me with a horse and gun, which he did. Putting Emma and Ida in charge of Mrs. Wakefield and others, with the request that they be forwarded home the next day, I bade them good bye and joined the party for the search.

There were but six or seven of us, not a very formidable party to encounter Chief Joseph, but we expected that Howard's troops were closely following the Indians and that they had ere this left the neighborhood of the geysers. We rode until twelve o'clock that night, when we came to an old man's cabin by the road side. Here McPherson, one of the party, suggested that we stop for the night and we dismounted. I immediately went into the cabin and sat down in a chair. That is all I remember until eight o'clock the next morning when I awoke and found myself lying on the floor on some blankets. The boys told me that I had fallen asleep as I sat down, and that they had picked me up and laid me out. I was completely exhausted.

We traveled Thursday all day and overtook Doane's party at Butler's Ranche that evening. To Doane I gave all the information I could relative to the Indians.

Here we learned that Jack Stuart had arrived by ambulance during Thursday night and reported Indians at Hot Springs. Duncan and Wilkie had come down also, leaving Detrich and Ben Stone at the springs, while Wickart and McCarty went back to bury Kenk and search for Joe Roberts and August Foller, the only members of the Helena party not accounted for.

Detrich and Stone had remained at the springs, as Detrich said he would not return home without Roberts. Roberts was a lad of eighteen or thereabouts, and Detrich had promised his (Roberts') mother that he would be responsible for his safe return. He, therefore, remained at the springs waiting and hoping that Weikart and McCarty would bring some tidings of him.

On Friday morning we pushed ahead for the Hot Springs, and in a few hours we came in sight of Henderson's Ranche. We found the ranche burning and could see the Indians on the side of the mountain beyond. Doane gave the order to push ahead as rapidly as possible and we reached the ranche soon after. It was then in ashes and the Indians having seen or heard us approaching, had taken to the mountain.

We encamped for the night and Doane ordered some Crow Indians and soldiers to the springs to rescue Detrich and Stone. The party dispatched returned about dusk and reported having found Detrich's body which was warm and bleeding. He had received four shots, one passing through the heart. The Indians that had fled from Henderson's burning ranche, were probably the ones that had shot him. Ben Stone was nowhere to be found. That night the soldiers and citizens did picket duty.

During the night Ben Stone came into camp, and as rapidly as his scare would permit, he related his experience about as follows:

Sterling Henderson, and "Loot" Crowell, started on the back trail for Bozeman.

We had gone but a little ways down the river when we saw some of the Crow Indians following us. I called Doane's attention to them, with the remark that we should have crow for supper unless he called them back. Loot Crowell also told him to call them back if he had any use for them. Doane did so, and the last we saw of them he was addressing them in language that was remarkable for its force rather than grace.

We made Emigrant's Gulch by night, where we were nicely entertained. We took an early start for Bozeman, but just before arriving there we were told that Joe Roberts and August Fo'ler had returned safely to their homes. Poor Detrich, he had unnecessarily forfeited his life in waiting at the springs for Joe's return.

On reaching Bozeman, I learned, with greater delight than I can record, of the safety of Dingee, Arnold, Myers, Mann, Harmon, and Oldham. All accounted for but poor George. After the amount of censure I had heaped upon myself, you can imagine how joyfully I hailed the tidings of the safety of the boys.

They were unmarked with the exception of Oldham, who was badly wounded in the face.

He subsequently related his adventures about as follows:

MR. A. OLDHAM'S ACCOUNT.

"We were riding along, surrounded by the Indians, Cowan being first, Ida next, then myself and then Mrs. Cowan. I had my gun, you remember, which they allowed me to retain as I had but three cartridges for it, and they had none to fit it. Well, all of a sudden an Indian rode down in front of us, drew his horse back on its haunches and fired at Cowan. At the same time the one that was riding on the upper side of me, turned loose at me. I felt a twinge in the side of my face, and tumbled from my horse. I fell in a ravine, but immediately jumped to my feet, and saw that the Indian who had shot me was following me. I grasped my gun and raised it to fire, and he started back up the hill. I snapped the gun but it was not discharged, which was certainly very providential, as, had I have shot him it would have been all up with the balance of the party. I was bleeding freely from the wound in my face, the blood running down my throat and over my vest. I found that the ball had penetrated the left cheek, and, passing downwards, had cut the tongue and come out beneath the jaw on the right side. The wound was very painful.

"You know it was lively times for the next few minutes, but during the time I kept my gun on the Indians, and they kept out of my way. I saw a lot of them go down to where Cowan was, and I then dropped down in the bushes and laid there until Saturday night, thirty-six hours from the time of the shooting. My sufferings during the time were intense.

"Saturday night I crawled out and went down to where Cowan was, or where I supposed he was, but he was nowhere to be found. I saw Mrs. Cowan's side-saddle laying in the trail, but could find nothing of you, Emma or Ida, whom I supposed were all killed. I thought, should I find you, I would pile your bodies in a heap, and cover you with brush and trees.

"Failing to find any of you, I went down to where some Indians had built a camp fire the night before, and got a fire brand, with which I made a fire in the woods and warmed myself.

"On Sunday I went to Gibbon's Fork, and followed that down until I got into the canyon of the Madison, where I remained during Sunday. On Sunday night I traveled again. I killed a grouse that day, but I could eat none of it, as my tongue was swollen so badly it protruded from my mouth. It was with the greatest difficulty that I could breathe.

"On Monday night I crossed the Madison and hid among some willows on a little island, and on the following morning I saw some Indians on Gibbon's Fork. I watched them closely, intending, if they came near me, to try and kill one of them and get his pony. The ford was close by, and presently I saw two coming across. As they came closer I got up on to my knees, so as to make a sure shot, when I saw they were white men. I stood up then, but I could not speak, and could only make a grunting noise. They heard me, and, riding up to where I was, I motioned for a pencil, which they gave me, and I wrote what I wanted them to know. They camped near by, and began doctoring me up. After they got some sugar in my mouth, and about the roots of my tongue, the swelling began to go down, and I soon got so I could talk a little and swallow some food they had prepared for me. They then moved on to Howard's command, where I found Arnold and Mann. I remained with the troops until we struck the Yellowstone, when I left them and came on to Bozeman, and here I am, not so good looking, perhaps, although I sport a fashionable lip."

As he finished, Dingee came in and saluted him heartily with, "*Al., how's your Little Bunch of Roses?*"

On Thursday afternoon, I was standing on the street in Bozeman, thinking of what course to pursue, as regards Cowan, when I saw a horseman coming down the street at the top of his speed. He was evidently on business of importance, and as he came tearing along, his horse foaming with sweat, many hailed him, but he responded to no one. He came directly towards me, and on reaching me stopped, and said:

"COWAN IS ALIVE!"

I could not believe it, and so told him. He said two scouts had just come into the post, and reported the finding of Cowan on the Thursday before. I hastened to the telegraph office close by and asked the operator to send no word of the finding until I had investigated farther. I then asked the courier for his horse, and started for the fort, but I met the two scouts, who told me that they had found one George F. Cowan and had talked with him. I returned with the utmost haste, and telegraphed the glad tidings to my brother at Helena, who immediately started with the news to Emma.

Soon after I heard that Shrively had escaped and was then up at the Lachede Hotel. I immediately repaired thither and as I came near I saw a dense crowd gathered about the door, seemingly intent on something going on within the office. Securing a position on the steps where I could see in, I saw Shrively mounted on the counter narrating his adventures. Turning around he saw me, and making a spring, lit in the crowd, and shoving them aside he came to me, I think there could be no heartier hand-shaking than that which followed. His adventures having been published, I will not refer to them.

On Friday morning I left Bozeman for home, arriving there about two P. M., shortly after Mrs. Cowan had received the news of Cowan' safety.

We left home the next morning for Helena and spent the Sabbath there. As yet we could not hear by what route Cowan would be brought home, so Mrs. Cowan remained in Helena that she might hear by telegraph the sooner, as it was thought by some that he would come by the way of Bozeman, and others thought that he would come by the way of Virginia City.

On the evening of Wednesday, the 19th of Sept., Mrs. Cowan received a telegram from Bozeman, saying that he had arrived at Bottler's Ranche on the Yellowstone, fifty miles from Bozeman. She received the news about ten o'clock, and at three A. M. she was *en route* to Bozeman, one hundred and twenty-five miles distant, where she arrived at 9 P. M. on Thursday evening. She took supper, hired a livery rig, and in an hour from the time of her arrival, was on her way to Bottler's Ranche where she arrived at ten A. M., having made a drive of one hundred and seventy-five miles through a mountainous country, over rough roads, in *thirty-one hours.*

She reached Cowan on the 24th of Sept., nearly four weeks from the time when we had left him for dead.

The meeting that followed we leave to the imagination of the reader. It suffices to state that they arrived home on the 5th of October, a little over two months from the time of their departure.

Before closing this rambling account, it is but just to say that the pleasantries thrust at the members of the party, were in the spirit of fun, and with the belief that they and their friends would accept them as such. The "enormous appetite" of friend Dingee is rather suppositional, as he really was the smallest "eater" of the party.

As I write, the party are all at home, and all have fully recovered the effects of their scare. The wounded men are convalescent, and it is the sincere wish of the author that we may all meet again for another trip to Geyser Land.

GEO. F. COWAN'S ACCOUNT.

I was riding in advance of the balance of the party, with Mrs. Cowan, Ida and Oldham following close to me. Mann and Harmon were on foot leading their horses, and Frank I did not see. We were surrounded by the Indians, although there were not many in front of us. The woods were full of skulking Indians and they kept coming and going constantly.

We had entered the timber and had gone but a little ways when looking up the trail I saw a number of Indians riding towards us rapidly. They came on a tearing gait until within eight or ten feet of me when they suddenly checked their horses, causing them to rear back on their haunches. I felt a twinge in my thigh and heard the report of a gun. I knew that I was wounded and sprang from my horse. I heard my wife scream, and looking up saw her spring from her horse. As I looked I saw the flash of a gun near Oldham, and saw him fall. I started to run into the bushes in the ravine, but my leg was benumbed, and striking a log I fell upon it close to a tree standing near it. As I fell I turned over and rested on my left elbow with my head down the mountain. The Indians gathered around me, and I saw my wife break through the crowd, run to me and kneel by me. She says:

"O, George! Where are you hurt?"

"My right leg is shattered," I replied pointing to the wound which was bleeding profusely.

"What will they do with us?" she asked.

"Be brave; keep up, Emma. If we have to die we will go together."

The Indians had gathered about us in a dense crowd, all talking and jabbering at once. I heard Ida scream and Emma rose to her knees. Ida continued screaming, when Emma rose to her feet and called for her to come to her. Ida came to us screaming at the top of her voice. Emma told her to be still, and she ceased. They both then knelt by me and my wife put her arms about my neck and began crying again.

Presently Charley, the Indian who had come into camp in the morning, came to me and said:

"Where you shot?"

Pointing to my wound, I replied:

"Me shot in the leg, Charley, you take me along. Me all right. Me get well."

I was now very thirsty and observing Frank near I asked him to get me some water. He made some reply that I did not understand. I remember then of calling for water several times. I saw Frank pulled back through the crowd. Just then Charley stooped and said:

"You no shot in here?" pointing to his breast.

"No, me shot here," I replied pointing to my leg.

He then drew the revolver that he had taken from Dingee, but my wife jumped and grasped his wrist, and then followed a struggle between them, she trying to hold the revolver in the air and screaming:

"Kill me first! Kill me first!"

"No, kill old one first," he replied, and nodded towards me.

There was considerable excitement among the Indians, and I could hear them say, "kill, kill."

During the struggle I turned my head and glanced up the trail, and as I did so I saw an Indian kneeling with a revolver within about three inches of my face. The next instant there was a flash, a deafening report, and a faint scream from my wife rang in my ears. My head felt as if a great weight had fallen upon it and crushed it, and everything became dark.

In about two hours I began to come back to life, and as I did so my head felt benumbed. The feeling as near as I can express it was a buzzing dizziness, and the sensation increased as it grew lighter and lighter. I began to feel, soon, and then my reason came back to me. My head felt very large, seemingly as large as a mountain, and I mechanically raised my hand and began feeling my face and head. I found my face covered with blood and my hair clotted with the blood that had cooled there. I then realized the incidents of the day and remembered the shooting. I could not at first discover where I was wounded, but after getting the blood out of my eyes and pulling my hat off with hair and skin sticking to it with the clotted blood, I discovered that I was shot in the face and head. Running my hand over my head, I found great gashes in the scalp, and I then thought the ball had passed entirely through my head in some way.— Feeling my leg, I found it completely benumbed, but that there were no bones broken. I again felt the intolerable pangs of thirst and raised myself on my elbow and looked about me. I then found that I was some ten or twelve feet from the place of shooting, and thought that the Indians must have dragged me after the shooting. This, I thought, accounted for the wounds in the back of my head. As far as I could see, the Indians were all gone and I could hear nothing but the moaning of the wind in the trees.

Standing near me was a little pine tree the boughs of which I could just reach, and grasping one I pulled myself to my feet. My wounds were very painful now. As I raised up I saw an Indian close by me sitting on his pony quietly watching me. I turned to run into the willows close at hand. The Indian observed the movement and started down toward me. As I was hobbling away, I glanced backward and saw him on one knee aiming his gun at me. Then followed a twingeing sensation in my left side, and the report of the gun and I dropped forward on my face. The ball had struck me on the side above the hip and came out in front of the abdomen.

I thought that this had "fixed me" beyond hope of recovery,

and I lay perfectly motionless expecting the Indian to finish the job with the hatchet.

I must have lain here fully twenty minutes expecting to die every moment, and during the time I think my mind must have dwelt upon every incident of our trip. I supposed my wife had not been killed. I knew the fate to which she and Ida would be subjected, and my whole nature was aroused as I thought of it.

Directly I heard Indians talking. They were coming up the trail, and I could hear them driving a number of loose horses. They passed within forty feet of me, but I was unnoticed and they were soon out of hearing. I waited for a few moments, then turned over and took a look around me.

I now took another inventory of my wounds, and in trying to rise found that I could not use either of my lower limbs. They were both paralized. I then turned upon my face and began crawling by pulling myself with my elbows, I thus managed to get into some willows where I found water which I drank eagerly, and felt greatly refreshed and strengthened. I now began crawling as before pulling myself on my breast with my elbows. In this way I crawled to a little stream of warm water, and raised up on my hands and entered the water. I immediately sank to my shoulders in the mud, and the water came up to my chin. This would not do, so extricating my hands, I again began crawling as before, and found that I thus could cross it. Having crossed it I entered the willows on the bank, and began crawling down stream and followed it until I struck the East Fork about a half mile below where I started from. It was now about one or two o'clock in the morning and being completely exhausted I lay down and rested until day-break.

At dawn I again started and crawled until noon, when I again stopped to rest. I had been here but a few moments when I again heard Indians approaching, coming down the trail. They passed within ten feet of me and were soon out of hearing.

I lay here for an hour or so and again resumed my wearisome journey. By night-fall I had made four or five miles, and I kept on during the night, resting at short intervals.

My wounds were very painful and were bleeding profusely, yet they did not bother me so much as the intense cold. The loss of blood, and the want of nourishment gave me but little power to withstand the cold. My clothing, too, was saturated with blood, and the mud and water cooling upon me seemed to take all the heat from my body. I was compelled to keep moving to keep up a degree of warmth.

I kept on down the trail, or rather by the side of it, and Indians kept passing by me every little while, driving ponies as they went. I could hear them approaching and then I would lie down and wait till they had passed.

I kept this up until Monday morning, having crossed the East Fork Sunday night, and reached the wagons that we had abandoned on Friday. I had crawled about nine miles in sixty hours.

As I approached the wagons, I saw some papers fastened upon the trees, and on going closer to them I saw that they were Mann's sketches made on the trip. I discovered portions of Frank's journal, and on crawling around I managed to pick it all up. I supposed then that I would die here, and I thought that the journal would tell them of the party and its capture. I also found Frank's pocket book, and many other articles scattered about in confusion. The Indians had attempted to destroy everything, and had even cut the spokes from the buggy wheels for stalks for their whips.

As I reached the wagon I found my faithful kog, Dido, laying beneath it. I called to her, and she came bounding to me, and covered my face and wounds with caresses. The pleasure of the meeting was mutual.

The buggy was laying upon the ground, all the spokes having been taken from two of the wheels, and I could search it without rising. I found some rags, and a portion of a man's underclothing, which were very acceptable, but I could find nothing to eat.

It occurred to me that I had spilled some coffee when in camp, on Thursday in Lower Geyser Basin, and calling my dog we started for it, I crawling as before, and the dog walking by my side. The coffee was four miles distant, but I thought not of that. The only idea was to possess the coffee. I was starving.

While crawling along close to the trail, my dog stopped suddenly and began to growl. I grasped her by the neck, and placed my hand over her nose to keep her from making a noise. Peering through the brush, I saw two Indians sitting beneath a tree but a few feet from me. I began moving back cautiously and made a circuit around them, keeping the dog close by me. I thus avoided them, and reached the Lower Geyser Basin on Tuesday night.

Here, as I anticipated, I found some coffee and a few matches. I found about a handful of coffee, and, placing it in an empty can that I had found, I pounded it up fine. I then got some water in another empty can, that had contained molasses, and building a fire, I soon had some excellent hot coffee that refreshed me greatly. This was the first refreshment that I had taken for five days and nights.

I now began calculating my chances for being picked up. I would not starve, as I could, as a last resort, *kill my dog and eat it.* I shudder now, as I think of sacrificing my noble, faithful dog; one that money cannot purchase now, but circumstances were such that I did not view it then as I do now. The natural desire for life, will force one to any necessity.

I remained where I was Tuesday night. No one can imagine my thoughts during that time. I supposed that I was the only one of the party left, unless it be my wife, and the speculations upon her fate almost set me mad. It was horrible. All night long I lay there suffering instead of resting, and I hailed with pleasure the break of day.

I made some more coffee and drank it, which seemed to give me renewed strength, but as my strength returned I felt more keenly the horrors of my position. I thought now I would crawl to where the East Fork empties into the Fire Hole River, so calling my dog I began my journey. I found that I was gradually growing weaker, as I could now crawl but a little ways when I would be compelled to stop and rest. At about a mile and a half distant I came to the place of our first night's camp on entering the basin. Here, again, I had to cross the river, but as the water was not deep, I made it without mishap. Here I rested for a few moments, before starting for the timber, which was about a fourth of a mile distant. I got there about two o'clock in the afternoon, and laid down under a tree and some brush close to the road. I was now exhausted and could go no farther. It was an expiring effort, and having accomplished it I gave myself up for dead.

In about two hours, I heard the sound of horses coming, but so completely tired out was I that I did not care whether they were Indians or not. My dog began to growl, but I did not try to stop her. The horses drew nearer, and approached and stopped. The riders had seen me. I looked up and saw that they were white men. They alighted and came to me, and one of them asked:

" Who are you ? "

I replied that my name was Cowan, and I asked them if any news had been received of my wife. They replied that there had not been, and I then cared for nothing further. I turned from them and would have been glad to have died.

One of them kept talking to me, and asking questions that I cared not to answer, while the other built a fire and made some coffee for me. They told me that they were scouts from Howard's command, and that the troops would reach me some time during the next day. They left me some " hard-tack " and a blanket, and went on to the scene of the massacre to find the bodies of the party. After they were gone and I had eaten, my desire for life returned, and it seems the spirit of revenge took complete possession of me. I knew that I would live, and I took a solemn vow that I would devote the rest of my days to killing Indians, especially Nez Perces.

I laid here until Thursday afternoon, when I heard the sound of approaching cavalry, and shortly afterwards General Howard and some of his officers rode up to me. In a few moments I saw Arnold coming. He came up, recognized me, and knelt beside me. We grasped hands, but neither spoke for some minutes. I could only gasp:

"*My wife!*"

"No news yet, George," he replied. He added that Oldham was with the command, and that Mann, Harmon, Dingee and Myers had gone to Virginia City. He said:

"Frank and the girls may get out all right yet; keep up George."

Arnold examined my wounds and told me that there were three or four physicians in the command, and I expected to have attention immediately.

Howard and staff now mounted their horses, and saying they would encamp near there, left Arnold and myself together.

Soon an ambulance came up with Oldham, and they lifted me into it. We went ahead a little ways and went into camp. Arnold lifted me out and laid me beneath a tree on some blankets, and went in search of a surgeon.

I cannot thank any of Howard's surgeons for my recovery, as Arnold could get no one to come to see me. One would send him to another, and he finally learned that they had all gone off with Gen. Howard to see the geysers. The general and his staff were picnicing while settlers were being killed or dying all around them. Arnold returned disgusted.

About eleven o'clock the general (?) and the officers returned, and one of the surgeons came to me. He grumbled about it not being his place to look after the wounded, and he began probing my wounds in anything but a gentle manner. He pronounced no bones broken, and with a pair of forceps extracted the pistol ball from my forehead, where it was imbeded in the skull. Arnold then dressed my wounds, Mann and Oldham rendering such assistance as they could. The soldier boys, also, were very kind and did all they could to alleviate my sufferings.

The next morning a courier came in from Bozeman, bringing the more than joyful news of the arrival there of my wife, Frank and Ida. This revived me more than all the attention I could have received. Before I was despondent, now everything wore a diffcrent aspect, and I could laugh and joke with all. The bright anticipations for the future, when my wife and I should be united, kept me up during the trials and sufferings of the days following, and probably did much to keep death at a distance.

In conclusion, I wish to say that I feel that A. J. Arnold saved my life. Without his care I do not think I could have lived. Others were kind ; he was unremitting in his attentions.

(For further particulars, see Arnold's account.—AUTHOR.)

A. J. ARNOLD'S ACCOUNT.

During the "swapping" that was carried on by the Indians, Poker Joe, or White Bird, pointed out a large grey horse standing near the woods, and told me to go and get him. I started to do so, and he went with me. Reaching the horse, he placed his hand on the saddle to see if it was on well, and then turned to me, and, putting his hand on my shoulder, said:

"You get'm in woods. Stay in woods. No get'm in trail again. Go quick;" and gave me a shove into the timber. He shook me by the hand as he did so, and I got into the bushes as quickly as I could, then stopped and looked back to see what was going on.

Down below me I saw Dingee walking backwards and leaning a horse around a marshy place, while an Indian followed him. I expected to see Dingee shot, but the Indian seemed to be waiting for the others to commence the killing. The rest of the party began to move, and the Indian stopped and looked around. I then spoke to Dingee and told him to leave the horse and come with me. The Indian then turned again, but Dingee was gone. They saw us, however, as we started, and fired five shots at us, but we were in the thick timber, and they had but little chance of hitting us. The woods were full of fallen timber and sapplings, and following us with horses was out of the question.

We ran up the hill about two hundred yards, and sat down to listen, and see if we could hear or see anything of the balance of the party, but we could see no one and hear nothing but the yelling and hooting of the red devils.

We sat here for some time, but as we could hear nothing, we concluded that they were all killed. I consulted my watch, which the Indians had not found, it being worn beneath my jumper, and saw that it was three o'clock.

We now considered the course to pursue. We were one hundred and fifty miles from any house, and a rough mountainous country to traverse. We were decided, as regards one thing, that was, that no other Indians should get us, if we had to walk five hundred miles. We started ahead, and by nightfall had made Gibbon's Fork. We thought it would not be safe to make a fire. I had matches, as I had placed some in my pocket in compliance with the advice of Houston, a few days before, who had told me never to be without matches in the woods. As we had neither coats nor blankets, we amused ourselves that night by crawling over fallen trees to keep warm.

At daylight we started down the river and traveled till about noon when we stopped to get dinner. Just how this was to be done was a mystery at first, but Dingee suggested that I go to the river and try my luck fishing. It then occurred to me that I had a line in my pocket, and we soon had three small fish baked at a fire Dingee had made in a gulch where the Indians could not see it. They tasted well after a two-day's fast, but Dingee's would not stay down. He was very sick for a time, and has never tasted fish since. He got so after a time that water would not remain on his stomach, and did not eat a bite for the next four days.

We reached the canyon of the Madison on the evening of the second day, and it was now necessary that we proceed with the utmost caution as the Indians would probably be watching the pass. We could avoid it by crossing a rough range of mountains, but concluded to try the canyon, and keep a good look-out ahead.

We began the descent, keeping in the bushes, and we soon discovered five horses grazing on the mountain side. We stopped, and by shifting our positions slightly we saw five Indians sitting beneath a tree. The only alternate left us now, was to scale the mountain, which we did almost in the face of the Indians, but as it was near sundown they did not see us.

By the time we had made the summit of the mountain it was night, and the air being extremely cold we were compelled to travel all night to keep warm. We made poor headway, however, as the woods were full of fallen timber, and the mountain was cut by deep ravines. When daylight came we were still in sight of the geysers.

We traveled all that day, but very slowly, keeping on the mountain range, and at night reached a little stream that flows by Prospect Hill on the road from Henry's Lake to the Basins. That night we suffered severely as it was extremely cold and so dark that we could not see which way to go. During the night I ascended a mountain to see which way to go, and left Dingee to wait my return. In returning I got lost, and wandered about a long time before I returned to him. On my return I found that he had built a fire, but as it was in a ravine I did not see it until I got close to him.

I was very weak and tired on my return, and sat down by the fire and dropped asleep. I awoke suddenly and found my clothing on fire. This would not do, so we began traveling again over fallen timber and through ravines until daylight. We then struck out on our course again but made little headway however, our progress at every step being impeded by fallen timber.

That night we reached the main pass of the Rocky Mountains on the Madison road. Henry's Lake lay upon the other side of the mountain and we thought that could we reach this we would find succor.

The idea of again scaling the mountains in our exhausted condition was discouraging in the extreme. We concluded to try the pass and emerged into an open space on the road, and stopped to take a good look ahead before venturing farther.

A glance at the mountain side was sufficient to decide us; three Indians were sitting near a camp fire guarding the pass. I said to Dingee that we must cross the open space, which was about one-fourth of a mile in diameter, and reach the mountain. He was opposed to the plan as it would reveal our presence to the Indians. I thought not if we could go fast enough, and we started. We were weak and tired, but if there was ever good time made on that course it was in that particular instance. I was surprised at Dingee's speed and bottom.

Then came the tug of war,—scaling the mountain. We made it by twelve o'clock, and as it was starlight we could see Henry's Lake below us.

As we looked we saw three camp fires. This was encouraging, as we thought they must be friends, and we would get something to eat. Dingee was hungry.

At daylight we began the descent, and as we left the mountains, we could see the camp fires lighting up in different places. I then thought we had struck another Indian camp, and was discouraged. We pushed on to reconnoiter, however, and as we approached, we heard a strain of the most beautiful music that I ever heard. It was a bugle call. We had found the soldiers. We traveled lighter now, and entered the camp soon after breakfast.

It was Howard's command, following Chief Joseph's Indians, that we had found, and imagine our chagrin when we learned that the Indians we had seen in the pass, were Howard's scouts, Dingee swore.

Harmon had beaten us in, but he thought the rest of the party were dead. Dingee got a conveyance to Virginia City, and carried the news that only three of us were saved.

After I had eaten sparingly, I went to Gen. Howard, who had sent for me, saying he wished to talk with me.

Our conversation was about as follows:

" How far are the Indians ahead of us ?"

" About seventy-five miles."

" We do not want you to go back. We will look after your party and things."

"I am going back any how. I want to see what has become of the party. I have walked four days and nights without food, and can do it again if need be."

"What were you doing in the Basins? Prospecting or trapping?"

"We were there for pleasure."

"You ought to have known that the Indians were coming."

"So should Gen. Sherman, then. Was he there prospecting or trapping?"

Our conversation closed with that, and I started back with the command.

The second day from the lake, we encamped at the Big Canyon of the Madison, and that evening we found Mr. Oldham. He had been found the day before by some of Howard's scouts.

That night Gen. Howard got a dispatch from Lieut. Schofield, saying, among other things, that Frank Carpenter and sisters had come into his camp on the 27th.

The next day we came to the Lower Geyser Basin, where we found Cowan. The news of the safety of his wife was hailed with joy by him.

Cowan was a most pitiful looking object. He was covered with blood, which had dried on him, and he was as black as a negro. His clothing was caked with dry mud, and his head looked like that of a tar-headed Indian in mourning for the dead.

The ambulance soon came up, and we placed him in it with Oldham. The surgeon told me that he would dress his wounds as soon as we could get into camp. We had but a short distance to go, and when we encamped the soldiers gave us blankets to make Cowan a bed, and we soon had him as comfortable as we could. The surgeon did not come, as he promised, and I went in quest of one, but could find none. At sundown I went again and saw Dr. Fitzgerald, who said that Dr. Hall was the one that should look after Cowan. However, Fitzgerald said he would go, and soon came over. He seemed to be angry, and did his probing, I thought, in a manner not in keeping with the wounded man's condition. During the operation of probing and extracting the ball from his forehead, some of them held a blanket up to secure Cowan from the wind, and to keep the candles from blowing out.

After the probing the surgeon left us, saying that it was not his place to dress the wounds. I then, with the assistance of the boys, washed and dressed the wounds as best I could, and some of the boys gave him some underclothing. The officers of the command offered us nothing, although they were supplied with everything. Neither Cowan, Oldham, or myself were in anyway indebted to the surgeons or the officers for anything.

Cowan wanted to be forwarded home by the way of Henry's Lake, but Howard said that in his condition he needed the best of medical attendance, (which was true), and that he would see to it that he received it, and that he would send him to Fort Ellis, (which was untrue). The treatment that he received and the attention shown him was to be placed in an old wagon and jolted over the worst road that ever was passed over by a wagon. The officers and surgeons would have let him rot alive. Some of the teamsters gave him underclothing, that was of great service to him, as his wounds discharged a great deal.

During our encampment near the basin, there would not have been an officer or a surgeon captured by the Indians, in case of an attack, as they were all off visiting the geysers. I suppose Howard was "prospecting or trapping."

The next day we passed the wagon and buggy that our party had abandoned, and found that they were almost totally destroyed. We gathered up what we could, and carried the pieces with us.

Arriving at the foot of the mountain that lies between the Yellowstone and the Lower Basin, the wagons stopped, but the cavalry and infantry went on to the Mud Wells. We, who were left behind, were well protected that night, as there was not a gun in the whole outfit.

The next morning the teamsters got out early to get up their horses, as they were afraid the Indians would get them. About nine o'clock the quarter-master came back and asked for them, and I told him where they had gone. He asked me to get upon his horse and go in quest of them, as I was not so heavy as he, and said that he would stay with Cowan.

I mounted his horse and started after them, but met them returning without the horses. They said the Indians had them. We were then compelled to send ahead for the pack mules, by the help of which we made the top of the mountains. Here we learned that our horses had been stolen by the Indians of Howard's command, they having left him at the Mud Springs and gathered up all the loose horses they could find before starting. Had it have been the Nez Perces what a delightful situation we would have been in.

That afternoon we made Alum Creek, and went from there to Mud Springs, where Howard was encamped. Here the cavalry brought in the Indians that had stolen the horses, they having been dispatched after them as soon as the theft was discovered. Howard turned six of them loose, but said he would keep the rest prisoners until the horses were brought back. The horses were produced forthwith.

Here we remained a day and a half, or until the arrival of scouts, who reported that the Nez Perces were coming back, and would probably go down Clark's Fork to the Crow Indians. We then moved to the Yellowstone that afternoon, and the next day went on to the Lower Falls. The roads were simply horrible, and almost impassible for wagons. At times we were compelled to lower them over precipices with ropes, and again we would hitch a rope to a wagon and pull it up the hill by man power.

Below the falls we had better roads, but, nevertheless, we were nine days going eighteen miles, by the aid of sixty sappers. Cowon suffered intensely, but bore it all bravely. Part of the time he was standing on his head, and then again he would be on his feet. It was enough to make a well man sick.

In Lower Creek we had a big scare. The teamsters lost two of their horses, and sent two men back after them. The men soon returned, and reported having seen about seventy-five Indians on the mountain. We thought then that the Nez Perces were coming back, and got things in readiness to give them a warm reception. We got the wagons together and put our guns in readiness to do the best we could by them. I told Cowan that I would go out and reconnoiter, and if they were coming I would carry him into the brush, as it would be necessary for us to get away the best we could. We soon learned, however, that they were Crow Indians, sent out by Lieut. Doane in search of Howard's command.

While on Lower Creek it rained so much that I could not get Cowan's underclothing dry, as he had to change every day. Cowan then sent to Captain Spurgeon, who had charge of the supply train, with a request that he would come to him. The Captain came, and Cowan told him of the trouble we had in keeping him clean, and asked him if he would sell him some underclothing. Spurgeon replied that he could not get at his. A man who was with him said the boxes were open containing the clothing, and that they could be easily got out, but the Captain refused positively to let him have any, and Cowan had to suffer. This was a fair sample ot Howard's noble-hearted officers. Noble, valorous Captain Spurgeon. As soon as he reached Fort Ellis he got uproariously drunk over his great achievments.

We soon came to a different lot of soldiers, under Colonel Gilbert and Lieutenants Dreuder and Scott. They were very kind, and willing to do anything that would be of a benefit to anyone in want, and we certainly needed their kind assistance as, from Burnett's Bridge to Fort Ellis, we all had a hard time of it, as it rained nearly all the way.

When we got to Bottler's Ranche, Cowan was too weak to rise, and it is a wonder how he lived at all. We had been carrying him in a Concord mud wagon for three weeks over the roughest road imaginable, and with little or no attention, more than what

I could give him, but I hadn't the means of alleviating his distress only in a measure.

At Bottler's Ranche Mrs. Cowan met us. The meeting of Cowan and wife can be better imagined than described. Their joy was too sacred for public perusal.

The fifth day after our arrival Cowan thought he could stand the journey homeward, as he had gained considerably in strength, and we started for Bozeman.

About seven miles from Fort Ellis we met with an accident that well-nigh put an ending to all our troubles. At this point the road is graded on the side of a deep canyon, and as we were going down it the strap of the neck-yoke broke, and let the pole of the carriage drop to the ground. About three feet of the pole broke and run into the ground, which caught the carriage and lifted it up into the air and tumbled us out, then rolled over off the grade and lighted bottom side up on the trees three hundred feet below us. The horses were thrown off the grade, but lodged upon the sides of the canyon.

We placed Cowan on some robes, and, on examination, found that his wounds were bleeding. We took a small can that we had, and, heating some water, dressed them again.

Soon a man came along with two horses, and our driver borrowed one of them to go to Fort Ellis for aid, and in about two hours came back with another team and a carriage. We succeeded in getting our horses on to the grade again, when we found they were much cut up.

We loaded up again and started for Bozeman, and arrived at the hotel about nine o'clock in the evening. We got Cowan some refreshments, and then went to dressing his wounds again. As we were dressing them the bedstead gave away and down went Cowan again. He got a fearful jolt, but looked up and innocently suggested "if we couldn't kill him any other way, to turn the artillery loose on him."

We remained ten days in Bozeman, and by the kind attention of every one Cowan regained rapidly.

On the eleventh day we started for Helena, seventy-five miles away, and made the trip in one day without exchange of horses.

With the sincere wish that we may all meet again in another excursion to the geysers during the coming fall, and that the day is not distant when our mutual friend, Charley, will give us a chance to liquidate our indebtedness to him, I close this narrative.

IDA CARPENTER'S ACCOUNT.

I was riding beside Albert Oldham a little ways behind George and Emma. The Indians were all around us. I saw two Indians on horses coming down in front of us at a full gallop. They stopped suddenly and fired, and George jumped or fell from his horse. At the same moment Albert Oldham dropped from his horse, being shot by an Indian a little ways above and behind us. Emma jumped from her horse and ran to Cowan, and the Indians made a rush and surrounded her and George. I sprang from my horse and started to run to where George was lying, with Emma kneeling by his side, but I was so terrified I could scarcely walk. I was benumbed all over, and the froth from my mouth was like paste. I thought certainly that I was soon going to be killed. I spoke to George and asked him where he was hurt, and he replied that his leg was all shattered.

Emma was kneeling with her arms around Cowan's neck, when an Indian came up, and, catching her by the hand, tried to pull her away. He pulled one of her arms from his neck, and then another Indian, seeing that Cowan's head was exposed, put a pistol to his face and shot him in the forehead. Emma fainted, then, and I jumped and screamed, and ran in and out among the Indians and horses. The Indians ran after me, and one caught me by the throat and choked me. I bore the prints of his fingers on my neck for two weeks. As he loosened his hold I had the satisfaction of biting his fingers.

They then put me on a horse behind an Indian, and we started on, leaving Cowan. I saw Emma on a horse, behind an Indian, in advance of us.

The Indians traveled on, driving loose horses with them. I cannot tell how terrible I felt. I had not seen my brother Frank only for a moment when he came up to where George was lying. I saw an Indian go away with him and I thought they had killed him.

I thought of my poor father and mother. What would they do, did they know of our situation. I could remember my mother's kiss as we parted, and her wish that we might enjoy the trip. I could remember father as he took us by the hands, and, kissing us, wished us a pleasant journey. I could see brother Willie as he stood at the door waving a farewell with his handkerchief. At that time I felt sorry for him that he could not go with us, as he would like to have done, but how I rejoiced now that he, too, was not a victim. I thought how fortunate that he would be left for father and mother. I thought of brother George, too, and his distress on hearing of our deaths.

I did not know what had become of the balance of the party, but supposed that they were all dead, and expected that Emma and I were to be killed soon, too.

It was quite dark soon, and I was very much afraid, as we traveled over high steep mountains, densely covered with dark pines. The wind sighed mournfully, as if in sadness for our fates. I never before heard the wind so sad and mournful. The Indians kept whooping and yelling at their horses, and the echo of their yells chilled me to the heart.

As we advanced the mountains became steeper, and I was forced to hold on with all my might to keep from falling off. I trembled with fear. I had read of savages burning their captives alive, and I thought this was why they were carrying us with them. I wished that they would kill us instantly and thus relieve us of our sufferings.

I had not seen Emma since we left Cowan, and we were now going into camp. Some had got there before us, and were sitting around their camp fires, and others coming in were in wild confusion, driving horses and whooping and yelling fearfully.

They took me to the middle of the camp, where there were a number of squaws and Indians of all ages. The squaws soon had supper, and gave me some bread, and tea made of willow-bark. The tea was so bitter I could not drink it. I could not eat, although they insisted on my doing so. They were very kind to me.

They made my bed on some buffalo robes, and the squaws laid down all around me, and thus watched me until morning.

In the morning I tried to see Emma but she was not be seen anywhere. I kept watching for her, and after a while I saw her on a horse that White Bird was leading. Oh, how rejoiced I was to see her. They let us talk together a little while, then took her back to another camp. She told me that Frank was alive and in camp. I cannot tell you how glad I was at this.

The Indians soon started again, and traveled until noon. Then a great many Indians went back to fight the soldiers. Soon after I saw brother Frank, and then the Indians held a council over us.

Reminiscences of Early Life in Montana.

In April, 1864, my father, D. D. Carpenter, and family started from the town of Black Earth, Dane county, Wisconsin, for Colorado. We were some weeks getting things ready to make the trip across the plains. My father had been across the plains some three or four times, but to his family, and especially myself, there was considerable novelty in the preparation and the forthcoming journey.

On the 28th day of April, 1864, we were ready to start. We hitched up our teams, and, on a bright pleasant morning, after bidding friends and schoolmates farewell, we started on our journey. I will here narrate some of the incidents, of which I recollect so well:

We crossed the Mississippi River, at Des Moines, and stopped there a couple of days trading horses and resting. We then resumed our journey, arriving at Council Bluffs about the 15th or 20th of May. Here my father and uncle, Thomas Logan, bought all their supplies and goods for the mountains, consisting of bacon, nails, whisky, sugar, etc., etc.

We left Council Bluffs, and drove on towards Omaha, and took our place in the line of teams or emigrants then crossing the ferry. As far ahead of us as we could see, or up to the bank of the river, stood a line of teams and emigrant wagons, and as fast as the ferry took over a wagon, the whole line of wagons would move up one wagon, or as many wagons as the ferry boat took across. My father's and my uncle's teams remained in this line twenty-four hours without unhitching our horses from the wagons, the while moving up as a wagon crossed the ferry, and so on until we arrived at the ferry. Then came our turn, with hundreds of wagons still in line behind us, and hundreds that had crossed before us. Having finally got our outfit across, we drove up into Omaha, and camped near the border of the town. We remained here several days, getting wagon tires re-set and so on, and about the first of June commenced our wearisome journey across the plains.

We got up to Columbus, the first town we struck after leaving Omaha, and situated on the Loup Fork. While crossing this river, Mr. Peck broke a wagon tongue, and this caused considerable delay. We finally fixed things all right, and again resumed our journey. Here it was we first came across Indians, they trying to stampede our horses while we were encamped, but without success. We followed up the Platte River until we came to Fort Kearney. Here my father intended to cross the Platte, on his way to Colorado, but after seeing two wagons and fourteen yoke of cattle go down out of sight in the Platte, concluded we would not cross at that ford. We then pushed on towards Julesburg, and after traveling several days got up near that point on the North Fork, and saw a man and family float off down the river in a wagon box, the water being so high as to float the wagon bed off from the wheels. The family, however, got out all right, I believe. My father concluded not to cross here, for some unaccountable reason, probably *family reasons*, and we continued our journey up to Laramie, where there was a ferry.

While encamped there on the river, the night before crossing, we observed hundreds of teams *en route* to the new gold mines in Idaho, and the people all going in that direction. Our party now got the fever, and after considerable argument, proposed that our crowd should vote whether to go to Colorado or Idaho. My father's interests were in Colorado, but after the majority concluded to go to Idaho, he consented to let his Colorado interests take care of themselves, at least for the present, so we remained here several days preparing for a longer journey. While here several soldiers from Fort Laramie came over and wanted to buy whisky, and as they offered $2.50 per quart for it, my father commenced business. After disposing of about ten gallons at this rate, the officers at the fort sent over word forbidding us to sell any more liquor to the soldiers, so that stopped business for awhile. My father and party now crossed the river to the Laramie side on a ferry, paying five dollars per wagon for crossing, the ferryman giving us tickets to cross at the bridge up the Platte from Laramie, two hundred and fifty miles, tickets being good for ferryage, bridge crossing, etc.

We found letters from friends and home at Laramie, and they were welcomed by our party. We again set out on our trip, and after one day's drive, camped for the night about thirty miles from Laramie. Early next morning a party of officers with some soldiers rode up, and my father was considerably uneasy, as he thought they had come on to arrest us for selling liquor to the soldiers after they had bidden him not to, but he was agreeably surprised to find that they wanted twenty gallons more of that whisky, at ten dollars per gallon, which emptied one barrel. They bade us farewell and drove off, taking the whisky in small kegs, and leaving the barrel there. After we had got away two or three miles, on looking back, we could see five or six soldiers around that barrel washing it out and drinking the water. Some of our party remarked that he would bet those soldiers would not leave that barrel as long as it smelled of whisky.

My father bought a mule at Laramie, and when we got up the next morning we saw that mule striking out for home, and two or three miles away, but that did not detain us, as father remarked, "let him rip. I wouldn't go ten feet for him, anyway." We were soon on the road again, and arrived at the bridge a few days afterwards, and found our tickets for crossing of no account. But, on our crowd consulting together, we concluded we would cross anyway, and when the crowd we were with made up their mind it did not take them long to act. We expected a fight, but the military concluded it would be wise to let our crowd alone.

After this we continued on up to the South Pass, overtaking trains that had been captured by Indians every day or two. As yet we had no trouble. We arrived at South Pass on the Fourth of July, where we had a dance and jollification. At Smoke River our party separated, some going to Idaho and some to Montana, my father among the latter. We arrived at Stinking Water, eighteen miles from Virginia City, on the fourth day of August, having been over three months crossing the plains and mountains. Many incidents occurred on the journey which, however, I will not attempt to describe here; suffice it to say, we were glad our journey was ended.

We rested here a week, and on the following Sunday my father went up to Virginia City, leaving mother and several of our party camped on the river. He got into Virginia City about noon, and, while eating dinner at a restaurant, asked the proprietor what he would take for his outfit, meaning the restaurant and appertenances. The fellow said, twenty-five hundred dollars. Father said, "all right; *I'll* take it." The proprietor said he would have to consult his partner first. Father said he would give him twenty minutes to decide, and if he concluded to take it to call on him at the city meat market, down the street two hundred and fifty yards. Father went down to the city market, sat down on a stool, and asked the fellow dishing out meat if he owned the shop. The fellow said he did. Father asked him what he would take for his business—shop and all. He said, fifteen hundred dollars. The twenty minutes was up, and father said he would take it, and half an hour later was dishing out meat to customers. The proprietor of the restaurant came in, and said he would take the amount offered, but father told him he was in the butcher business, and would supply him with meat at the usual rates—eighteen cents per pound.

Father done business a week, and then came down after the family, and we moved up to Virginia City, on Alder Gulch, a gulch thirteen miles long, and, at that time, was paying five, ten and fifteen dollars per hand, on every claim, and employing about eight thousand people in and about the mines and city.

The gulch, or parts of it, are still being worked, but Virginia City of '78 is not the Virginia City of those days. At the time we arrived it was a scene of wild disorder. The Vigilanters were in session most of the time, and hanging, shooting and rioting were the common events of the day. To look at the quiet streets of Virginia one could hardly imagine that thirteen years ago it was a scene of such wild acts.

The winter of '64 was a hard one, and provisions were scarce, though money was plenty. During the latter part of winter and in the April following, we had what was called the flour riot. Flour went up to one hundred and twenty-five dollars per hundred pounds, and could not not be bought at that. It was not there to buy.

The gamblers, rioters, and prize fighters took matters in their hands, and determined to make a raid on the city and get all the flour in it, and a couple hundred of them started at the business, but soon let the job out, as the citizens would not endure a mob like that pillaging the city, and after the shooting of one or two of them they dispersed,

The miners next took up the raid, and one morning, at about ten o'clock, there came five hundred armed miners, gathering recruits as they marched along, some carrying flour sacks in their hands, and one carrying a banner, made of flour sacks, on which was written, "Flour or Death." Merchants and all surrendered at the approach of this body of men, and then commenced a scene of wild confusion. Miners, men, boys, gamblers, and all sorts of people joined in this cry for flour, squads of five, eight, and ten going through different houses, gathering what flour there was, and carrying and depositing it in a large two story building, intending to divide it with the citizens and miners that were in want. In some places they would find half a sack, in others two or three sacks, but in the majority, by far, they found none.

I shall never forget their coming into father's house in search of flour. Father had gone over to Lost Chance, (or Helena now), one hundred and twenty miles from Virginia City. We had been keeping the hotel called the Wisconsin House, but had failed during the winter. Just before father left, he had bought a sack of flour at one hundred and twenty dollars, and had told mother to take care of it, as flour was becoming impossible to get. Mother deposited this flour in a box we had taken a melodeon through in, covered it up with a sheet and placed a lid over the whole.

I had been up on the house-tops on Main street watching the rioters, and enjoying it only as a boy can, when I thought mother would be frightened if they came into our house, so, crawling down off the house-tops, I got back home and found mother all alone. She commenced asking me what all the noise in the streets was about. I told her the people were after flour, going into everybody's house and taking it. I had just finished speaking when in came eight miners, armed with revolvers and shot guns.

Coming up to mother, the spokesman said:

"Madam, we are compelled to search this house for flour, and, although it is a disagreeable task, we will have to do our duty."

Mother was crying and somewhat frightened at these fellows but she said, "all right;" and they commenced searching the kitchen. Mother and I sat in the dining room, I sitting on the flour chest.

The men looked hurriedly through the house, and, in passing through the dining-room, one of the men said:

"Madam, we can find no flour here, so you may send your boy down to the big building on Main street, and we will send you your share."

My mother thanked them, and they started out. Just as they got to the end of the dining-room, one of them stopped and said:

"We did not search the box that that boy was sitting on."

I was considerably frightened during all this time, but as he came up close to me I said:

"You don't want to search my mother's clothes press, do you?"

He said he did not, and turned and followed the others out.

After they had gone, I said: "Mother, we fooled them plenty; didn't we. Now, you just bet, I'll go down and get that ten pounds of flour," and I did. Mother gave me credit for a little smartness.

The flour riot was a success, and after finding several hundred sacks, the flour was divided among families and miners. Those that had money paid for those that did not have it. Some paid fifty dollars for ten pounds; others paid fifteen or twenty dollars, according to their pile of wealth. I have heard that W. F. Sanders offered two hundred and fifty dollars for one hundred pounds, at the time of the riot.

One merchant, who was suffering from hunger, said: "My poys, I don't have got no flour, only shust a leedle bit in my sthore. I knows you no find any more as dot leedle sack."

The boys, however, went out back of his store and tipped over a hay stack and found, hidden beneath it, twenty sacks. The expression on that merchant's face can be better imagined than described.

After the flour was divided, a committee of the rioters went around and paid all merchants fifty dollars per sack for what had been taken from them, which was a good profit, as the flour had cost to get it there, about ten dollars per hundred pounds—freight and all.

In the fall of '64, political excitement ran high, and at the time Col. McLane was elected to Congress, and during the time of electioneering, it was lively. Col. W. F. Sanders was McLane's opponent, and lived next door to my father's. McLane stopped at the Planter House, on the opposite corner. The brass band would play "Dixie" in front of the Planter House, then cross the street and give us "Yankee Doodle." Between the tunes, drinks would be sandwiched. It may be remarked that all hotels and restaurants kept a bar in those days, and as far as I am able to judge, do so yet. Either without it would quietly drop out of existence in two weeks, for lack of patronage.

Next door to Col. Sanders' was the printing establishment of a small paper called the *Montana Post*. In the course of two months the building was vacated, and was used as a house of worship. Next to this was a large saloon, and next came a large gambling saloon, and adjacent to this was a " hurdy-gurdy" house. On the opposite side of the street was an auction store, and all of these stood within fifty yards of the Wisconsin House, of which my father was proprietor.

On Sundays all these houses were patronized, and it would bother a listener, standing on the steps of our house, to tell which made the most noise. The preacher, gamblers, auctioneer, and " hurdy-gurdy " outfit, all shouting at once. A few free fights in the street, with pistol shot accompaniment, was no unusual occurrence during the progress of the exercises. Perhaps there was never a place on the earth where there was such a commingling of the good and the evil, with the latter largely predominating.

There was lively times among the hotels then, too, and each would vie with the other in securing patronage. It was a part of my duties on Sundays to stand in the dining-room a half hour before dinner and rattle dishes, that the public might *hear* that we were doing a large business. It drew, and we generally had about a hundred and fifty for dinner on that day.

In the spring of '65, my father went over to " Last Chance," or " Helena New Diggings," that had just been struck, and bought out a restaurant. He sent word for my mother, Emma, Ida and Willie to come over on the coach, and left my brother George and I to pack up the household goods and come over with the ox train. When he purchased the restaurant, he had, also, bought some fifty pounds of flour, but this soon gave out and he was compelled to quit business, as he had not learned the art of conducting a restaurant without provisions.

While in Virginia City my father had formed a partnership with a German named Mauer, a slow, easy-going kind of a fellow. He also packed up his goods and loaded them on the same ox train upon which we had loaded our goods, and set out with us for the new diggings. About a week or ten days previous to our going, he had shipped to father one hundred pounds of salt and other commodities for immediate use in the restaurant. He opened a store in connection with his restaurant, with the salt as a basis. He had the good fortune, too, of buying half a sack of flour for seventy-five dollars, and my mother having made it into pies, he added a bakery to his establishment, and did a thriving business, as he retailed the salt at one dollar and eighty cents per pound, and the pies for two dollars and twenty-five cents each. The pies, particularly, were in demand, as a long file of men were in waiting for their turn to get the pies they had contracted for before being baked. The profits on all was about six hundred and fifty dollars.

We arrived in about three weeks after this, and found that the family had been without flour for almost two weeks, and had been living on beef alone. But we had brought a sack of flour with us, and soon had matters to rights again.

Father now commenced business in earnest, as Mauer had a pretty good stock of goods. Mauer had an ox train loaded with flour, that had been snowed in on the other side of the range towards Ogden City. It arrived in Helena about the middle of June. Before its arrival in town Mauer said to my father:

"Carp., take that flour and do the best you can with it."

Father asked him if eighty dollars per sack would satisfy him, and he replied:

"Yes; or seventy-five dollars either."

Father then told him to keep the train out of town three or four miles until he wanted it. He then got some posters and hand bills printed, stating that he could furnish all with flour at one hundred and fifteen dollars per sack, and started my brother, and myself, and about a half dozen others, to distribute them among the miners. On Saturday evening, Mauer brought the train into town, and on Sunday morning we were ready for business, with five hundred sacks of flour to dispose of. Other dealers came to father, and offered one hundred and twenty and one hundred and twenty-two dollars per sack for the lot, but it was not for sale to them at any price. About nine o'clock the miners began coming, and by night we had sold four hundred and ninety sacks.

We had done more than this, as we had thus secured the trade of the miners, which we kept during the summer. Father bought out Mauer's interest in the store, and paid eighty-five dollars per sack for the flour. During the next five months we did business to the amount of sixty-two thousand dollars, the trade being confined to vegetables principally. Potatoes sold for sixty cents per pound after the eyes were taken out, which sold for one dollar and fifty cents per pound for seed.

The morals of the place were about on a par with those of Virginia City, as we had the dance houses, gambling saloons, etc., with all that the names imply. The miners would come down on Saturday night, and, after settling the store bills, would go to a gambling saloon or the "hurdy-gurdy," where they would remain until Monday morning. They would then return to their work, and on Saturday night come down again for a repetition of the same. This they kept up during the entire summer.

Sometime in July the citizens indulged in their first "hanging bee," and one John King was the victim. While sitting in front of my father's store one day, King and another man passed by. King seemed to be talking earnestly to his companion. They passed on up Bridge street, until opposite Sam Green's gambling saloon, where they stopped. King drew a revolver from its sheath and, turning toward the saloon, fired three shots at a man sitting on the door-step, and killing him instantly. The first shot struck the man in the forehead, and the others took effect in the body. King then put up his revolver, and, turning to his companion, continued his conversation at the point where it had been broken off. They stood thus talking until interrupted by C. D. Curtiss, who approached King and said:

"Here, Cap., I want you!"

King turned to the man with whom he was talking and said that he would see him again, and, handing his revolver to Curtiss, started down town with him.

They came down the street to a lumber yard, and placed him on a pile of lumber. One of the citizens asked him why he had shot the man, and King replied that they were old acquaintances, and, having quarrelled in Blackfoot and parted with the mutual agreement to shoot on sight, in case they met, he (King) had "got the drop on him." That was the defense. The citizens took a vote to dispose of the case, and in a half hour afterwards King was swinging from a limb on "hangman's tree," on the edge of the town. This was one of the many similar occurrences during the summer and winter following. It is entirely different now, most of the rough element having gone to the Black Hills, where the same scenes are enacted as at Virginia City and Helena.

Perhaps a few remarks as to the methods of mining may be of interest to those who have never witnessed the processes. I will take Diamond City as an example of hydraulic and placer mining. This city is situated about forty-five miles from Helena, and has produced more gold in proportion to the size and length of the gulch (called Confederate Gulch) than any other gulch in the territory.

The mouth of the gulch is about eight miles from Diamond City, which is situated above. The road winds up the gulch between very high mountains, so high in fact, that it is a common saying that one must look twice to see the summit, being too high for one look. Boulders, gullies and prospect holes of all sizes and without numbers, are encountered as one picks his way carefully through the gulch, and a ride of eight miles over such a road brings us to a sudden turn in the road beyond which lies the city.

The only street runs along the gulch, and the miners' cabins, hotels, saloons, livery and feed stables, line its sides. It is about six hundred yards long and about twenty feet wide, and is not noted for its picturesqueness nor beauty. The gulch at this point is about fifty or sixty yards wide, and back of the houses are the mines, and the main street is tunneled underneath. Here we see hydraulic mining.

A ditch runs along the side of the mountain hundreds of feet above where the miners are at work, that comes from the head of streams and catches the water from the melting snow at the summits and holds it as a reservoir for mining purposes. The water is conducted from this ditch by the means of a large canvas hose, about eight inches in diameter, that is laid on the surface of the ground, and winds in a serpentine course down to the gulch.

The gulch end is fitted with a nozzle two to three inches in diameter, and the water rushes through with such an immense force that it, on being turned against the mountain, knocks dirt and boulders in every direction. During the time that the water is playing against the bank, a smaller stream is flowing from another ditch a few feet above the top of the bank into the sluice boxes, into which also empties the stream from the hose with the dirt and stones that it has washed from the bank. The dirt and gravel is carried through the sluice boxes by the water, and at the lower end is dumped. As it passes through these boxes, however, the gold that it contains is separated by a process described further on, and remains in the riffles.

The sluice boxes are made of foot lumber, and is composed of a bottom and two sides. They are generally twelve feet long, and are carried down the gulch as far as the miner wishes. The lower end of each box fits into the upper end of the one below. In the bottom of one or two of these boxes is what is called the riffles, which are made of a board full of two-inch auger holes, and then fitted into the bottom of the sluice box. A small quantity of quicksilver is placed in each hole and the water now turned in at the head from the small ditch. The hose is brought to bear against the bank, and the muddy water, gravel, and stones, among which the small particles of gold is mixed, passes into the sluice boxes also. As the water passes over the riffles the gold, which is much heavier than the gravel, etc., drops into the holes in the riffles. The quicksilver then adheres to it, making it still heavier, and thus prevents its being washed out.

In cleaning up the water is turned off, and the gold dust and quicksilver is brushed into a gold pan. It is then panned out by washing the dirt out of the pan, leaving the gold dust and quicksilver in the pan. It is then dried by putting the pan on the fire. If the miner wishes to save the quicksilver he places the contents of the pan in an iron crucible which is fitted with a tight lid, and has an iron pipe about three feet long attached. The crucible is then placed in a forge, like a blacksmith's, and heated to a melting heat. One end of the iron pipe is placed in a tub of cold water, and as the quicksilver is melted, it passed out through this tube in the semblance of vapor. As the vapor touches the cold water, it becomes condensed, and falls into the bottom of the tub in the form of quicksilver and is again ready for use. The gold which remains in the crucible is now taken out, and is called "retort," and is generally worth more than other gold, since the melting has freed it of many impurities.

Those miners who do not use quicksilver, catch the gold in the riffles, pan out the dust, dry the gold, and it is ready for market or use.

Placer mining consists in *shoveling* the dirt into the sluice boxes, instead of using the hydraulic power, or in sinking a shaft to the bed rock and hoisting the dirt to the sluice boxes. But this method of mining as well as of hydraulic mining has gradually been superseded by quartz mining, which now may be said to constitute the mining interests of the territory.

Quartz mining is done by crushing the rock that contains the gold and silver before the washing process.

A prospector, in climbing over the mountains, generally strikes a lode by observing the croppings, which is a line of rock running up the side of the mountain, and is about six inches to a foot in width. By the use of the pick and shovel he soon throws up enough to determine its character. If he thinks it is good he still sinks farther into the lode until he has attained the depth of ten feet or such a matter, and then definitely determines its value by getting a piece of rock assayed, which gives its value in gold or silver to the ton of rock. If it is so rich and there is a quartz mill convenient, he commences his mining operations in earnest by sinking a shaft lengthwise of the lode and blasts the rock with powder. He then hoists the rock to the surface, and carries it to the mill, where it is first broken into pieces about as large as a hen's egg, with a sledge hammer. It is then thrown into the feed box of the quartz mill, or crushing machine.

The mill has generally five stamps that weigh from five hundred to one thousand pounds each. There is a revolving shaft across the tops of the stamps that is so attached that it lifts them alternately and lets them fall upon a block of solid iron. Inclosing the lower part of the stamps is a square box in which the crushing takes place. At one side of this box is a tin screen made of a sheet of perforated tin. A rubber hose carries water into the top of the box, and as the stamps crush the quartz into a fine dust it is washed through the small holes in the screen out on to copper plates that is covered with quicksilver, which catches the particles of gold, and permits the refuse rock and dirt to pass off into sluice boxes. The plates are brushed off, and the mineral therefrom is called bullion.

There are two kinds of lodes, viz.: silver lodes and gold lodes, the name being determined by the predominating mineral found. The quicksilver is separated as before, and the mineral then becomes either retort or silver bullion. It is then shipped by express to the United States Assay Office, at Helena, where it is melted and run into square bricks. It is then assayed and found to contain so much silver and so much gold, and stamped with its value in silver and in gold, and also with the fineness of each, nine hundred fine being about the average for Butte silver.

Leaving Diamond City we go up the road until we reach a trestle work under which the road passes. Looking up to the right, on the mountain side, we can see the ditch from which the water is obtained for the hydraulic mining It is eighteen miles long, and is four feet wide by three feet deep. This ditch carries the water for the mining on the other side of the gulch, and below us, and it is necessary that it be brought across the gulch to another ditch on the opposite side, whence it is carried by the hose to the mines below. This is done by the means of an iron pipe two feet in diameter, that is laid down from the first ditch, across the trestle work, and up the mountain on the other side to the second ditch, where it empties its waters. The owners of this ditch and some of the mines took out a million and a half dollars worth of gold dust. But Diamond City, like many others, are numbered among the things that were. They have the wealth if they only had the money to develop it.

The principal mines of Montana are at Butte, Helena, and Strawberry, near Virginia City.

Montana is destined to be one of the richest territories of the west. Its mines cannot be excelled, and its farming lands produce forty to fifty bushels to the acre of wheat and barley. Thousands of acres are waiting to be tilled, and its ranges for stock are unsurpassed. Stock lives the year round without feeding, grazing on the ranges and in the valleys always being good. Beef and game are always found in abundance, (and Indians also).

In closing this volume I can but reiterate the advice of Horace Greeley, with this amendment, don't let the Indians catch you.

www.ingramcontent.com/pod-product-compliance
Lightning Source LLC
Chambersburg PA
CBHW022113160426
43197CB00009B/1002